T5-ASD-593

The Actor's Guide
to Qualified Acting Coaches
LOS ANGELES

Other books by Larry Silverberg,
published by Smith and Kraus
The Actor's Guide to Qualified Acting Coaches: New York
The Sandford Meisner Approach: An Actor's Workbook

Smith and Kraus *Books For Actors*

CAREER DEVELOPMENT: Technique

The Camera Smart Actor
The Great Acting Teachers and Their Methods
A Shakespearean Actor Prepares
Anne Bogart: Viewpoints
Nikos Psacharopoulos: The Master Class
The Actor's Chekhov
Taken To The Stage: An Autobiography by Mimi Kennedy
Auditioning For Musical Theatre
The Actor's Guide to Qualified Coaches: New York
The Sanford Meisner Approach: An Actor's Workbook

CAREER DEVELOPMENT: Actor's Guides

The Job Book: 100 Acting Jobs for Actors
The Job Book II: 100 Day Jobs for Actors
What to Give Your Agent for Christmas *and 100 Other Tips
    for the Working Actor*
The Actor's Guide to Promoting Your Own Career
Hot Tips for Cold Readings: *Some Do's and Don'ts for Actors at Auditions*
The Smith and Kraus Monologue Index

If you require pre-publication information about upcoming Smith and Kraus books, you may receive our semi-annual catalogue, free of charge, by sending your name and address to *Smith and Kraus Catalogue, P.O. Box 127, One Main Street, Lyme, NH 03768. Or call us at (800) 895-4331, fax (603) 795-4427.*

The Actor's Guide
to Qualified Acting Coaches
LOS ANGELES

by Larry Silverberg

Career Development Series

SK
A Smith and Kraus Book

A Smith and Kraus Book
Published by Smith and Kraus, Inc.
One Main Street, PO Box 127, Lyme, NH 03768

Copyright © 1996 by Larry Silverberg
All rights reserved

Manufactured in the United States of America
Cover and Text Design by Julia Hill

First Edition: February 1996
10 9 8 7 6 5 4 3 2 1

CAUTION: Professionals and amateurs are hereby warned that the material represented in this book is fully protected under the copyright laws of the United States of America, and of all countries covered by the International Copyright Union (including the Dominion of Canada and the rest of the British Commonwealth), and of all countries covered by the Pan-American Copyright Convention and the Universal Copyright Convention, and of all countries with which the United States has reciprocal copyright relations. All rights, including professional, amateur, motion picture, recitation, lecturing, public reading, radio broadcasting, television, video or sound taping, all other forms of mechanical or electronic reproductions such as CD-ROM and CD-I, information storage and retrieval systems and photocopying, and the rights of translation into foreign languages, are strictly reserved. Particular emphasis is laid upon the question of public readings, permission for which must be secured from Smith and Kraus, Inc.

Library of Congress Cataloging-in-Publication Date

The actor's guide to qualified acting coaches. Los Angeles /
[edited] by Larry Silverberg
p. cm. --(Career development series)

ISBN 1-57525-010-1
1. Acting--Study and teaching--California--Los Angeles.
2. Acting teachers--California--Los Angeles--Directories.
I. Silverberg, Larry, 1959 – . II. Series.

PN2078.U62L672   1996
792'.028'02579494--dc20   96-2434
CIP

Acknowledgements

To Helen Rooney, my wife's mom, who transcribed the hundreds of hours of taped interviews, this project would have been impossible without you. Thank you for your wonderful and thoughtful assistance. You amaze me!

Contents

Introduction

Why This Book

I am very excited to bring this book to you. Whether you are an acting student in search of the most appropriate teacher for yourself or you are an acting teacher interested in discovering the philosophies and approaches of some of our countries finest teachers, I believe this book will serve you well.

I began the book, motivated by a recent experience I had with an acting student from out of town who came to meet with me. She had heard about my work through my acting book on the Sanford Meisner Approach and she called to see if I would coach her for an upcoming audition. We met at my theatre and as we worked, she reached a place where she could not go on; it was hard for her to breathe. She got very quiet. She looked down at the old rug on the floor and she began to weep. She went on to tell me that she was a dancer who was now shifting into acting and that she had just quit an acting class back in her hometown after attending it for a year and a half. The class was her first acting class, and the teacher, her first acting teacher. She went on to tell me ugly stories of being humiliated, emotionally abused and violently manipulated in the classroom by her teacher. I was horrified and deeply sickened. Of course, we hear stories like this all the time about psycho-therapists, doctors, ministers and others who use their position of power to carry out their own warped desires. It's always shocking, isn't it.

The acting teacher plays a crucial role in the lives of their students. Serious acting students come hungry to learn the vital skills which will bring them closer to realizing their dreams of expressing their most private voices. And to learn this craft, students must be willing to be guided by a mentor and by a process that will, hopefully, lead them in a healthy and organic way into the unknown. For the unknown is where all great theatre springs from.

Thus, the acting teacher must hold sacred the trust the students offer. The teacher must hold to the highest integrity, always championing for the highest good of the students. The teacher must be like an arrow, always aimed at the goal of teaching the skills that will lead each student towards discovering and improving their own, individual craft of acting. The acting teacher must not turn the learning space into a therapy session or an emotional war zone. The acting teacher must not "break" the student or abuse the student in any manner. The acting teacher must guide the students in such a way that the students become not more like the teacher, but more the expression of who they themselves truly are. The teacher must be a great listener. The teacher must be fully available in each moment so as to learn from each student what that student most needs. Finally, the teacher of acting must model simplicity, generousity and humanity in the classroom; for these are the deeper components of the art of a true theatre.

Putting It Together

I thought you would like to know how I went about creating the book. First, I held lengthy interviews with each teacher. These interviews were audio taped, transcribed and then edited. As you will see, I have taken out all of my own questions and comments; I felt it would be much more interesting to present each teacher in the form of a personal "monologue." You will also notice that I didn't go in there and fix up the grammar. Personally, I'm not into neat and tidy, I enjoy how people really talk. So you are getting the teacher's words, not my interpretation. And, I interviewed many more teachers than appear in the book. Each teacher was also required to choose a number of students that would respond to a survey I created. This survey asked the students questions about their experience in the classroom with the teacher and what in their work together has been most valuable. The responses to these surveys were mailed by the students directly to me and then edited. Finally, The teachers who appear in this edition of the book are simply the teachers who, after talking with them and reading the statements sent in by their students, I felt best about presenting to you at this time. I hope to bring you many other wonderful teachers in future editions.

The final stages of this book have been coming together in an extremely busy time for me. I have just finished up an acting class I have been teaching and this past Friday, I opened the play SHIVAREE which I directed at my theatre here in Seattle. (By the way, you must read this beautifully rich play by William Mastrosimone. Quick, go get his collection of plays, also published by Smith & Kraus!) But throughout the process of creating it, this book has been a joy for me. I have had a chance to get to know some fabulous people and artists; teachers who are caring and generous, thoughtful, intensely interested and who are doing such great work with their students. So often during the interviews, I'd find myself wishing I could drop everything and go study with them. And then to read the passionate and loving comments of the students who shared so personally with me. Powerful! I was moved over and over by their feelings of how their acting teacher had helped them to discover and open new doors of authentic expression; that the work they had done in the classroom had led them to see the world in a more vivid and alive way; and that they considered their acting teacher to be one of the greatest gifts in their lives.

Now what

It's very simple. You wanna study? Go and meet these teachers in person. As many of them have said, go and see if the two of you click. I know this book is giving you a fantastic jump start on your homework, now the follow through is up to you. Don't get lazy on me! Listen, forget about the money, it's meaningless. Who you study with is about an investment of your life and your time—which are precious, you know?

Please let me know if you find this book useful and if you end up studying with any of the teachers in the book. I'd love to hear from you with your experiences. If you'd like to suggest any other teachers for future editions of the book, please send me their names and contact information. You will find my telephone number and address at the bottom of my Bio at the end of the book.

To all of the teachers and students who participated, thank you. I appreciate you so much!

To the reader, have a wonderful adventure!

Love, Larry

Chapter 1
JOLENE ADAMS

My first formal training started at Adelphi University with Jacques Burdick. He had come from the Yale University Theater Department and he was a brilliant man who really inspired me. He was very irreverent, but he made me feel like there was something very decent and beautiful about acting; that it was truly a noble art form. When I moved to New York, I met and studied with Martha Jacobs who taught a two-year Meisner program. The thing that I admired most about her was that she was an extremely dedicated teacher and very serious minded. Martha was really my most influential teacher because she taught me something so specific.

In my teaching, I know that each actor dictates their own curriculum because of their different needs and their level of commitment. Certain people come to me knowing what they need to learn; if they don't know, then I prod them to find that out. You know, a lot of students that say they want to be actors aren't really courageous enough, so they wind up picking teachers that won't ask them the right questions or won't bring them to a certain level because of their own fears. So, it's really the student that winds up asking for what they need, and I spend a lot of time in the beginning just trying to get the student to admit their commitment level. The most important thing to me in teaching an actor is to make them independent minded so that they are director- and writer-proof. If you have a great director and you have wonderful writing, the possibilities are just incredibly magical—but that rarely happens in the working world. So an actor has got to be analytical, vulnerable and incredibly focused. I try to teach a system that includes how to analyze the script as well as develops their imagination and receptive side so that through this balance, they can really be in control of their craft.

The first thing I do is teach students how to put themselves in a receptive state, which I call the alpha state. This is a state where you're susceptible and where you can be affected more by your emotions and everything around you. You know, this is a natural state that we go into a million times a day and it's a choice. If you're reading a book, you decide to put your body into a receptive state and you decide that you're going to be affected by that book. If you're watching a movie, you make the same decision. If you're having a conversation with a good friend, you make that decision. Once I teach them how to master that state, acting becomes a lot easier. Then I teach them my version of the repetition exercise which leads them to reading behavior, trusting their impulses and focusing their attention in the moment. It also gives them the basis of an improvisational structure, so that they can turn any scene into an improvisation.

Then I get into text analysis. They have to understand the basics: the cold facts the playwright's given, which they will need to make personal; what their character's objective is; what their character's focusing on at the first moment of the scene; what are the pleasures they're moving toward or the pain they're moving away from; and what's at stake. Then I teach them how to improvise from moment to moment so that they learn how to find the meaning of every moment and the beats, as opposed to finding the beats from their head, which is what I was taught in college. After all this work, I meticulously go through the text with them and teach them how to particularize and understand first the playwright's point of view of every subject that gets mentioned in the text, and then the character's point of view.

Next, I get to character work, and I teach them that all character comes from emotion. If you meet a person and you start talking to them, within about two minutes, you could tell what the basic emotion is that that person lives in. When you work on a role and you've spent two weeks fully immersing yourself in that person's reality, you'll start to feel the overall emotional essence of that person. In life, you might say of someone, "Oh, that person is basically sad." It's like a verbal statement comes out of people, "Oh, God, life is hard," or "I'm just so glad to be here." I believe that everybody has a basic emotion that's with them and that creates the tensions in their body as well as the mask that they show the world. So I teach them how to do character observations, which they then bring into rehearsal. Ultimately, you will find that if you are 100 percent relaxed and aligned, you will discover the character's tensions; it will affect your voice, it affects the way you walk, it affects the way you think—and all very naturally.

To me, you're not really acting unless there's somebody watching you. So I arrange an evening with invited guests where the students can perform whatever role they're working on in class and where they can really learn that when you let go of the "working on it," it takes on another whole life of its own. So performance is the final step to all the work—trusting it, letting it grow, and giving up the control.

My strengths? I love teaching and I love helping somebody "get it." I'm very flexible on how I present the work depending on the actor's temperament. I'm also a very good reader of character and behavior, so it's easy for me to know what somebody's thinking, as opposed to what they're saying to me. What I mean is, I can cut through a lot of garbage. I have a huge passion for teaching and connecting with people on a very deep level. In an interview with a prospective student, I try to find out what their past training was and what their goals are. I give them a little sample class. I'll give them a scene to read with me so I can see if I have something that I can give to them. And then I'll begin to work with them as a coach just to give them an idea of how I work and see if I make sense to them. I want to see in that one-hour interview if I can make a slight change in them for the better, and whether our personalities connect or not.

The Students of Jolene Adams

LAURA RICHARDSON
Jolene knows what you need to work on, where your faults lie and what your strengths are. She always communicates in a non-confrontational manner. If you're not getting it, she keeps trying new and different approaches or sets you on a course to discover your own approach. And Jolene gets me off my bottom and pushes me with her continual, unrelenting fervor and devotion.

Jolene is so positive and supportive. She encourages me to take risks, she tells me when I am succeeding and she relates with me as a creative peer who enjoys sharing the art of acting.

ANDREA TATE
Jolene has trained me in breaking down the script, looking for the clues to create a character and how to be absolutely present in the moment. She is clear, precise, intuitive, intelligent, caring and passionate about acting.

The greatest value I have gotten from working with Jolene is that she always has her students in workshop performances. This has allowed me to have real experiences and the opportunity to play a variety of great roles. In my professional work, I have received praise for my work and talent—I have only Jolene to thank for that.

ANN SCOTT

One of Jolene's most outstanding qualities is her ability to get the best performance possible from each actor. She will work with you as hard as you are prepared to work yourself. She is also a wonderful actor and living proof that the technique she is teaching works.

Jolene's classes are always exciting and great fun. Her energy and enthusiasm are something I found sadly lacking in many of the other acting classes I have taken over the years.

Jolene Adams: The Facts

Actor's Art Theatre Studio
6128 Wilshire Blvd., #110
Los Angeles, CA 90048
213-857-5891 (studio)
213-969-4953 (voice mail)

Length of time teaching: 12 years
Classes:
> *Script Analysis and Technique:* Call for schedule.
> *Rehearsal and Performance Technique Workshop:* Call for schedule.
> *Scene Study and Improv Workout:* Wednesday, 7:30PM.
> *Character Workshop:* First Saturday of the month,
>> 2:00PM – 5:00PM
> *Classic Sunday Workshop:* Last Sunday of the month,
>> 2:00PM – 5:00PM

Private Coaching: $40 per session; $120 per 4 monthly sessions
Admission: By interview and audition

Chapter 2
WILLIAM ALDERSON

When I finished college, I knew that I wanted to be an actor and I knew that I didn't know anything. So when I came to Los Angeles, I had an agent who sent me to Twentieth Century Fox to be interviewed by Sanford Meisner to be put under contract. He said, "You're really not a straight leading man type, so I can't get you in the talent department at Twentieth Century Fox." We sat there and neither of us said anything for a long time, just sort of sat there and every once in a while I would say something like, "Did you really teach Steve McQueen?" And so finally I left and I said, "I want to study with that man." I tried to save up as much money as I could to go back to New York to study with him, and I just couldn't. Something always happened. It took me another two years and finally, in February of 1962, I drove across country with a friend of mine and I started to study with Sandy. And I studied with him from 1962 well into 1965.

One day Sandy said, "You have a good way of putting things. I want to see you after class." And I thought he was going to say "Shut up. You talk too much," or something like that, but that didn't happen. He said, "You should be a teacher." And I was shocked. I said, "I don't want to be a teacher. I want to act." So he said, "Well you should be a teacher. You could teach." So he pursued me for a long time, years. Finally, I was out here in LA in 1967 and I get a call from him saying, "I have an opening as an assistant here at the Neighborhood Playhouse and it's yours if you want it, and I'm never going to ask you again if you don't take it." I said, "Well, can I have 24 hours to think about it?" He said, "Yeah." And I said, "You know, Sandy, I want to act." He said, "Bill, you can do both. I did." I said, "You know, that's the first time you've ever said that to me." He said, "Well, that's the first time I ever thought about it." So I went. I was also going back to do a play with Al Pacino which Joe Papp was directing. So I did the play and started teaching at the Playhouse, and gradually the teaching at the Playhouse just took over.

The Playhouse was very exciting, stimulating, and I was teaching, directing and sitting in on all of Sandy's classes. I admired Sandy's integrity as a teacher—he never sacrificed his integrity for one minute. He taught the things he believed in because he knew they were tried and true. If there was something wrong in what you were doing, he wouldn't accept it. His concern was always for the student. The biggest difference between Sandy's work and the other approaches is the working off of the other actor and leaving yourself alone. You've got to be wide open in order to really do that. The other techniques, especially the method, have nothing to do with the other actor; they don't have the working off of each other and they don't have the listening. I studied the method for two years from a teacher in New York and the other actors would be doing sensory or some kind of substitution work and they just weren't there with me, they weren't listening to me. It would infuriate me. We would be doing a scene and I wanted to break the illusion and say, "Why aren't you listening? I'm talking to you." Sandy worked with the Stanislavsky system and he took out everything that he didn't like and thought was nonsense, whether it's nonsense or not, he didn't like it because it didn't apply to him. He didn't like working from personal problems in acting and he didn't like the sensory work. He didn't like imaginary objects and he didn't like using dramatic experiences and emotional recall. So there's no bullshit in the Meisner technique because Sandy threw it all out. It's the most practical and the most thorough training you can get in a two-year period. No doubt about it.

In my teaching, the beginning work is to get students to listen and to be spontaneous and to scrape off the veneer of conventional acting; getting them to respond to each other quite freely. As those skills are strengthened you move into the activity work and the extension of the readings of the behavior. Then we carry the exercise work over into their first simple scene. After this, I start them on the emotional preparation work and making the independent activity more emotionally meaningful. We also start to work with relationships and more difficult and emotionally demanding scenes. I take my time with that. I am at all times trying to give the students an understanding of what it really means to live truthfully under imaginary circumstances and to get them to understand the difference between something in real life and something in an imaginary world of acting—which demands a greater truth. I am also trying to help them learn to be simple. It's hard to be simple. There's an English mystery writer who said, "Intellectuals don't understand truth, it's too simple."

When I interview students, I get a sense of where they're really at and what they're looking for. I'm looking to see if they are serious. I tell them that the nature of the work is difficult and that it's going to take a couple of years to really learn this technique, but once they have it, they'll really have something. Most people are in a hurry and looking for shortcuts. If someone's in a hurry, I can't deal with them. I think that the environment in my classroom is not a heavy one, which is a good thing for learning. Jeff Goldblum calls me a tough teacher, but if anything, I'm a little too lax sometimes. The only thing that I do not tolerate in class is if the students are talking amongst themselves when someone is working; I do resent that.

You know, having studied with Sandy and then working with him for 20 years as his assistant, and then as his associate at the Playhouse, I really know the technique. There have been what I consider three master teachers: Meisner, Strasberg, and Stella Adler. I don't consider myself a master teacher, but I do know that I know the Meisner technique and can teach it inside and out.

The Students of William Alderson

JANET ASPERS

Working with Mr. Alderson, I am learning how to get out of my head and into my real impulses, how to listen and how to be specific. I am also learning how to interpret according to my life experience, what a relationship means and what it is to be in the moment. Mr. Alderson has taught me a respect for acting and a joy for the craft. He has helped me discover the living, breathing, feeling person that is me, and how to bring that to a role.

Mr. Alderson is always forthright and honest in his responses. He doesn't put up with laziness or people's ego problems, but as long as a student is trying to do the work, he is patient and supportive. I appreciate that Mr. Alderson is a teacher who makes demands and he is a man of high integrity.

DON BLOOMFIELD

Bill Alderson shows zero tolerance for anyone who would attempt to lower the standards of his teaching or of his most dedicated students—God help that fool who would pace the back of his class while he gives extra time to a needy pair of scene partners. He is unsurpassed in his own dedication and he demands that we respect him, our partners and the work.

I have learned from Bill that the only way I will get anywhere is if I am willing to do the work. And that is the only thing he has ever asked of me.

KIMBERLY KELLY

There should be a warning sign outside of the William Alderson Acting Studio that says, "ONLY FOR SERIOUS ACTORS!" Bill tells you what you did right, what you did wrong and what you need to improve—PERIOD. To this day I have never gotten away with a thing in his class. If you haven't rehearsed—he sees it; if your preparation is wrong—he feels it; and if you are not being truthful in your acting—he knows it.

Bill treats each of his students like a different creation, a new work of art. First, he strips away all of your bad habits and misconceptions about acting. Next, he sands away the convoluted mind, leaving behind only a core of raw instinct. Then with the utmost care, he paints layer upon layer of fresh, uninhibited technique. Thanks to Bill, my work is no longer a product of luck, it has become a sixth sense.

William Alderson: The Facts

The William Alderson Acting Studio
821 & 3/4 Fairfax
West Hollywood, CA 90046
213-669-1534

Length of time teaching: 28 years
Classes: Call for current schedule
Private Coaching: $75 per hour
Admission: By interview

Chapter 3
GARY AUSTIN

I majored in theater at San Francisco State College and it was kind of an awakening for me because I came from a very sheltered upbringing in the Nazarene Church in Texas and Southern California. That was my small world. So when I went to college, I was not only awakened to theater, but I was awakened to literature, culture and the world itself. Tom Tyrell, a man of great dignity and knowledge, was my teacher and mentor there and he used to call me "the thinking actor." Well that became a big problem for me. I became so bogged down in intellectualizing my performances that acting became drudgery for me. So much so that I didn't want to be in the theater anymore and I became a social worker in Los Angeles.

But then The Committee from San Francisco opened a show at the Tiffany Theater on Sunset Boulevard. I just happened to be driving by and I saw their name on the marquee and it said, "Opening Tonight." I knew that my friend Chris Ross was in The Committee, so I went to the show that night. It was the first time I'd ever seen improv and I was completely blown away. When I found out they had a workshop, I joined it. Eventually, I was able to go on-stage and work with these incredible improvisers, many of whom had come over from Second City. I was an actor in The Committee for two years and that's where I really learned my craft. I went on to be part of The Comedy Store players in L.A. and we used to improvise with Red Foxx and Flip Wilson—everybody in show business came through there. It was at that time, in 1972, that I started to teach. And it was those first classes that eventually became The Groundlings.

In my teaching, I am trying to help people get to the intuitive, instinctive part of themselves, and that's very hard for people to do if they're adults. Children have no problem with that, they're already there. I help people to have a sense of trust of the people around them and to learn to trust themselves. I like to disorient people in the work, so that they have to stay in the present moment. In the games we play, I also emphasize behavior and emotion—which are not separate.

There is an exercise we do where a student learns the meter and the rhyme scheme of a poem and then the class members will suggest a topic. The student's task is to begin to improvise the poem immediately without thinking and never pausing until he believes he's finished the poem. Even if he gets completely lost, even if it becomes a non-poem, even if it becomes non-English, he must keep talking until he thinks he's finished. Now, if it rhymes, if it has the right meter, if it's English, if it makes sense, that's icing on the cake. What we're really doing here is taking away the results. The process becomes the goal. And everything we do in class is about the process of accomplishing the task as opposed to the result that we may want to see. Sometimes a student will turn to me and say, "Oh my God, my mind is blank." I say, "OK, now you can improvise." The ideal state to be in when you improvise is to be disoriented, lost, and blank.

I believe that the other actors are your greatest resource on-stage, and that you must be observing, listening and responding to them. In this way we are committing to the unknown every few seconds, we're jumping off the cliff before we find out how many feet down it is to the bottom. You know, I got to study with Del Close from Second City, and the most important lesson I ever learned from him was the fuck it adjustment. He said, "Just before I go on-stage, I say fuck it, and I maintain that attitude until I come off. Once I get off, I tear my hair out. But out there, it's fuck it." What that means to me is, you're going to fail sometimes. That's OK. Go ahead and commit to your work. If you fail, you fail. Look, the best home-run hitters strike out more than any of the others, but they also hit the most home runs. I even have exercises designed to help people to be, at first, artificially proud of failure. These exercises are almost impossible to succeed in; they are designed so that when you fail, you show us how proud you are of your work.

Largely, what happens in an improvisation—and it happens over and over and over—is something called "arbitrary choice." Say I suddenly point to the ceiling in an improvisation and for no reason go, "Oh, my God!" That's an arbitrary choice because I don't know what it has to do with the scene I'm doing. OK, the other actor looks at the ceiling where I'm pointing, and says, "It's getting worse." I then say, "That's right. The landlord refuses to fix the ceiling." And the other actor goes, "You want me to get a bucket?" So, starting out with the arbitrary choice, pointing to the ceiling and saying, "Oh, my God!" we add information until we justify my arbitrary choice by making it that the ceiling is leaking. So, in a sense, we don't have the feeling that we're creating this thing but that It has a life of its own and we are following it. There are three categories for an arbitrary choice. One is verbal, one is physical, and one is emotional. Usually they all three happen at once, but very often one predominates over others. An example of an arbitrary verbal choice would be, "It's happening again," and when I say that in the scene, I don't know what I mean. We then add information until we find out what it is that's "happening again." An emotional choice might be that I suddenly start to cry, having no idea why I'm doing that, and then we find out why I'm crying. And a physical one would be suddenly getting up out of my chair, walking to the fourth wall, once I get there making the arbitrary choice of opening a window, then making the arbitrary verbal choice of saying, "Get away from my car." The audience then understands or believes the illusion that you, the character, heard a sound while sitting on the couch of someone breaking into your car. So the illusion of improv is that the characters knew what they were doing before they actually did know. And we create that illusion every few seconds.

I think my strength as a teacher is the environment of support and trust I create in the classroom. Not only are we not judging you, but you're not allowed to judge yourself. We're certainly not going to be your censor and you can't be either. I say to my students, "There's only one thing you are not allowed to do here. You are not allowed to purposely injure yourselves or others or destroy property." I go out of my way to make sure that everybody understands that this is a safe place. When we get into the emotional stuff and you are making creative choices, you may offend someone or hurt their feelings. But it's the same rule, you're not allowed to hurt each other deliberately.

I am continually evolving my theories and my approaches based on what works and what doesn't work. You know, Del Close said something incredible the first day I ever met him. He got up in front of the class and he said, "I'm going to lay out a bunch of rules about improv and you must follow those rules. However, if you break a rule and it works, I will applaud you. If it doesn't work, I will castigate you, but you must feel free to break it at the risk of a reprimand." That certainly made a big impression on me and in my own teaching, I encourage taking risks and breaking the rules. If it doesn't work, stick to what does. If it works, GREAT!

The Students of Gary Austin

ROBERTA WALLACH

I have seen Gary work true miracles. He has patiently helped students through tremendous fears and blocks. I have seen extremely shy and closed people go into extraordinarily daring character areas with his guidance. The most important things I have learned from Gary are trust, spontaneity and fierce concentration. He has helped me more than anyone ever has with my audition technique and he taught me to make rapid and stunning choices in my work.

DOUG MANES

Some vital things I have gotten from my work with Gary are: honesty, point of focus, immediacy, trusting my impulses and staying out of my head. As I go through an improv, I know that Gary is completely dedicated to me and my work in every moment. He is a genius in his knack for knowing what's working, what's not working, and why.

Because Gary runs the class itself like an improv, every session is fresh and unpredictable and often, delightful. I know that when I go to his class, I'm in for a rewarding experience.

ROB WATZKE

Gary taught me to live in the moment, to hang on to it, to luxuriate in it, to get out of my own way, and for God's sake to stop thinking and start listening! The biggest impact Gary has had on me has been to make me feel that as long as I'm working truthfully in a scene, there's no way to fail. This has been incredibly freeing

It's very exciting to me that every time Gary says, "Two people go on-stage," seven or eight students will rush to get up there. It's a tribute to the atmosphere Gary creates that people feel safe enough to throw themselves headlong into the work. This is a great class taught by a sensitive teacher.

HELEN SLATER

After studying acting for many years, I felt constricted, self-conscious and tired of the feeling of competition among my peers. Through the improvisational work with Gary, I found I felt free again, available to play and be foolish and to commit to my choices without apology. For the first time, I understood how innovative and deeply creative actors could be.

Gary is a generous, non-judging teacher. No matter what level you're at, how far you've come or still need to go, his commitment to you and to your individual process is stunning. I cannot recommend him highly enough.

Gary Austin: The Facts

Third Stage Theatre
2811 Magnolia Blvd.
Burbank, CA 91505
818-753-9000
800-DOG-TOES (364-8637)

Length of time teaching: 23 years
Classes: Call for current schedule. (Gary also teaches workshops in New York and Seattle)
Private Coaching: $100 per hour
Admission: All students welcome

Chapter 4
ADILAH BARNES

I began acting when I was 16. I was in a college prep program called "Project Upward Bound" and my very first acting teacher was a man by the name of Larry Dick. I really credit him as being the first beacon of light as a guide, as a teacher, as a director. I went on to receive my BA in Theater Arts from the University of California, Santa Cruz. During that time, I went to Emerson College on a field study where I had another important instructor in my life, Sheldon Feldner. Later, I attended the American Conservatory Theater in San Francisco and I ended up going back to teach there and to join the company. I became the first African-American to teach full time in their advanced training program. Ed Hastings, the acting instructor at A.C.T. was my third beacon of light. I appreciated so much his sense of calm and fairness.

I believe first and foremost that every actor needs to train, even those that may be considered to be natural actors. Everyone needs to train whether they're interested in television, film, or stage. Even for those actors who want to do on-camera work, they really do need to be based in theater work. Every actor needs the experience of doing a play, preferably more than one play, even if that's not the medium that they're interested in. There's so much that can be gained in that particular medium by learning to be in the moment and by experiencing what it is like when there are no second takes. I also believe that actors must approach their work, first and foremost, from the text. And as a teacher, that's how I initially approach the work that I do with students—we go back to the text: we do the script analysis; we do the character analysis; we establish a sense of place and environment; we tear apart what those things are that motivate the character. So we look at the objectives, the actions, the obstacles, the stakes, the risks, and we create the biographies as we explore the intrinsic information that is in the text.

My class is composed of students of different levels and the one thing my students have in common is that they possess a passion for and a commitment to their work. To get into the class, each person needs to interview and I prefer that they audit before they interview so that they have a sense of me as a teacher. In the interview process, we talk about their background, where they see themselves at this point, where they want to go, which medium they're most interested in, what they see as areas that they need to work on and what they see as their strengths. These questions have to do with their craft, but they also have to do with their person. And we talk about why they want to take an acting class, why my acting class, how they'd like to challenge themselves and if they ought to be in the class. Then they have an opportunity to interview me. And then I conclude by taking a look at their prepared monologue. I find that looking at a person's monologue is extremely telling and oftentimes I can identify what areas that actor may need to work on, and also what that actor's strengths are. Then, if it's mutually decided, they actually take the class.

The class really incorporates many things. In the ten weeks, everybody develops one scene and one monologue. I'm not interested in students working on three to four different scenes in ten weeks—I don't know how in the world actors are able to create depth when they study that way. Also, as the students are working on the scenes, they are required to do written homework which supports their exploration of the material. In class, if people are stuck, I sometimes use improvisation and I always use a couple of theater games at the beginning of class. Since each actor is only working with one partner on one scene, through the theater games, they can work with their classmates in other ways. I also bring the world of the industry to the class so the two are merged. We talk about the students audition experiences during the past week and any offers of work they may have had. It's important that people know who's working in their midst because it's inspirational. And at the end of each week, I spend about twenty minutes talking about a specific aspect of the business. Finally, we conclude the class with industry night. So they're getting several things: they're getting the practical experience by working on the scenes and the monologues; they're getting the academic experience because they're doing the written homework; and they're having the exposure to the industry. Then they get the opportunity to do the industry night so there's a sense of performance at the end, although I like to think of what they do as works in progress. And because people from the industry come, students may actually receive either representation or the opportunity to interview with someone or they may actually get an offer to do a project. That I see as the icing on the cake because it's really about rolling up the sleeves and doing the work. If that match happens at the industry night, that's great, but that's not the focus. The focus is creating work of truth, of depth, and creating honest communication between scene partners and within the world that they reside in.

I think I have several strengths as a teacher. One is that I'm very perceptive and sensitive and I'm constantly aware of the dynamics that are happening at any given moment in the class. I'm tapped into each student and I know when to push and when to nurture and I know when to set limits if I feel like there are students in the class that are inappropriate in terms of how they're relating to others. I'm also analytical, and given that, I'm able to work with the students in that way by taking them back to the text, tear it apart and start from point A. And I teach from an actor's point of view because I am also an actor.

The environment in my class is one that is, in a healthy way, competitive and yet also balanced in terms of being nurturing. I try to create a sense of ensemble with the actors so that it's not about them competing against each other, but rather supporting each other. And where that competition lies is within the actor, the actor trying to be better than they were the week before. You know, I feel fiercely about my sense of integrity as a human being and as an actor. Hopefully, I influence students in terms of thinking about the bigger picture, about being selective in the work that one does, particularly in television and film because we're constantly creating an image of who we are based on the work that we choose. I truly care about developing actors. Actors are trusting and they're surrendering themselves to someone else to work with them and I take that responsibility very seriously. I'm not about beating people up and wounding their egos and making them dependent on me. I'm about being a guide and working with students in a way that they're able to actualize what they want; being a channel for them to make some discoveries that are going to help them stretch.

The Students of Adilah Barnes

ALMA COLLINS
Of greatest value in working with Adilah the past three years, has been the depth to which I have grown. She has helped me to take risks, expand the range of characters I explore and to "nail" my auditions. I am now able to take the stage while at the same time, giving to the actors I am working with.

Adilah is a gifted instructor; she is supportive, encouraging, insightful, nurturing and a wonderful director. She is always available with advice regarding auditions, finding an agent and whatever you need to improve your craft or advance your career.

MICHAEL RAWLINS
The one thing that has had the greatest impact on me is the way in which Adilah has taught me to access myself in order to bring greater depth to my work. I have learned that there is more to acting than the spoken word and that when I fill the unspoken moment, it will ring loud and true. Adilah has also trained me in breaking down the text, developing a character, choosing material that best highlights my talent and the business side of the industry. Also, Adilah is supportive above and beyond a teachers call of duty.

Adilah Barnes: The Facts

The Complex
6476 Santa Monica Blvd.
Hollywood, CA
818-752-2225

Length of time teaching: 17 years
Classes:
 Character Development Workshop
  Tuesday 7:00PM – 10:00PM
Private Coaching: $45 per hour
Admission: By interview and prepared monologue

Chapter 5
JACKIE BENTON

Elizabeth Rhienholtz, my high school drama teacher, was a major influence for me. Although she did not lead me to the specific technique that I teach now, what she gave to me is at the heart of everything that I do. Elizabeth was validating, supportive, dedicated, and she had respect for the people that she worked with. We were not treated as children, we were treated as professionals. She encouraged me and she helped me to believe in myself and to recognize the actress in myself. I then went on to graduate from the American Academy of Dramatic Arts in New York. I really didn't set out to be a teacher, but you know, "If you want to make God laugh, tell him what your plans are." So, I was in St. Louis in the mid-sixties and I was helping a friend who was in a play, and through the request of some other people, we put together an acting class. And over these last thirty years, I've incorporated all the things that I have used as an actress into what I feel I need to impart to my students. If I believe in something, I can teach it. If I do not believe in it through my own heart feelings and also through practical applications, then I have to go in a different direction. Also, I find that the lessons I have learned in the school of life (I'm not a youngster—I have two grown children and I'm about to be a grandma any second now!) have made me a better teacher.

My philosophy of teaching acting is to free the talent that is already within the individual. And in order to do that, I need to make my students aware of certain principles of acting that put them in touch with themselves, their own strengths, and their own creative power. I cannot teach someone to be creative and I cannot teach someone to be talented. Whatever potential the individual brings, that's what I am addressing. The end result of what I teach is extremely powerful and the means of getting there is very, very practical. The main principle in what I teach is that there is a creative process and that that creative process is available to all of us. And an example of that would be the work of Van Gogh, or when you hear a concerto that is particularly moving—that those great artists have tapped into that amazing, incredible, and ever present creative process. The second principle is that the character is in the script and I don't have to bring life to the character, she has a life of her own. I don't have to create the character, she is created. If I never pick up ROMEO AND JULIET, Juliet has a living presence and an energy and a form that is hers. And the third principle is that when I connect with that creative process, when I plug into it, the character is just there. By the way, the basic process that set me in this direction, was an extension of Sanford Meisner's techniques carried into cold readings, where you just get yourself out of the way and you connect with your partner.

So those are the three primary principles. Then that all sounds very good and well, but the question is, how do I connect with that creative process on a consistent, non-accidental basis. And we could put that into three steps. The first step is to get out of the way. The second step is to allow the character's experience to be there for you, to allow that into your body, into your feelings, into your heart. And the third step is to express that which you are experiencing. And the biggest step is the first step, getting out of the way. But there are inner blocks and there are outer blocks. Outer blocks might be misinformation or a lack of information. Our body could be a block, a physical block. For instance, I remember working with a student who by simply having him lower his chin, became very open. Now the inner blocks are mistaken information that we have acquired regarding ourselves, our creativity and our self-esteem. We lose touch with ourselves and we become out of focus. So by letting go of those inner blocks, we are open.

Now, once you are open, the second step is to allow the experience of the character in. So many actors will pick up a script and discover, if they are able to get themselves out of the way, that they know the character on a deeper sense. This will occur if they are able to suspend the thinking process so that they can respond to what is there and not what they think should be there or what they hope would be there. Suppose that the experience makes me uncomfortable, or suppose the character is a person who's not likable, an evil person. I have to tell you right now, that the thought of allowing in that experience of evil is not comfortable. But if the actor gets rid of the block to let that character in, then we get to the third step— expressing fully what I am experiencing. When it's over, it's over and I don't have to carry it home with me and live with it. I don't have to awaken elements of my emotional growth and past experiences that have been worked through and healed. So it's a very healthy and safe way to work and it's also non-personal. It isn't as if I were in this situation. I step aside, allow the character to be there and it's the character in that situation. So if I want to fall in love with my leading man, I'm in love with the character, not the leading man. So the non-personal element that is involved in this gives the actor tremendous freedom.

To get to the practical aspect of what I teach, the tools that I use are the techniques of cold reading, the cold reading itself, and group exercises. Cold reading is a means to an end and it's an end in itself. I want my students to be able to go in, pick up a script, read it through once, and do it. In order to be able to do that, the student has to learn how to not think. In most techniques, and when I do scene labs, I demand that the student do the thinking, breaking down the script, understanding the character intellectually, going through that search process that is so essential, having the ability to discuss it intelligently and making conscious choices. But in my cold reading class, which are for approaching film work, my students must learn how to not think, how to trust their talent and their intuitive processes. The first and most basic technique that the student has to learn is how to get words off the page easily and effortlessly. And to that end, I teach a sight reading exercise which the student must practice on a daily basis. What they're learning to do is to trust the potential that they have to not really read the words, but to see a word on the page and expose it to the brain. This has many benefits. One of them is, it keeps you from getting to a preconception and getting stuck in a cliche, because your attention is not on yourself—it is on another person. Therefore, you are open to the secrets and the unspoken words that are not written on the page, but are contained within every script. So it's not reading, "Gee, it's a really nice day." It's that I am connected to you. I look at you. A song fills my heart when I look at you. My feelings are there and the words are ready for me, "Gee, it's a really nice day."

So, here you are, you've been studying this process. Your agent calls you and says, "Gosh, I'm sorry to call you so late, I know it's twelve o'-clock, but can you get over to so and so at two o'clock because there's a perfect role for you. The casting director just called me and they want you to come over and read." So you go over and by the time you get there, you have sixteen minutes. You look through the script, you do not make choices, you go in and you do it. Your preparation for that script has been all the work that you have put in up to then. Now we come back to that wonderful little homily, "Luck is preparation meeting opportunity," and if you prepared for that opportunity, you can pick up that script and the character will be there for you and you will enter into true moment-to-moment acting. If you are simply centered, connected to your truth and open, and your focus is where it belongs, when someone says something to you, you will respond in that moment.

When I talk with new people on the phone, I can almost always get a clear idea of what their intent is. And what I want in my class are individuals who are intent on fulfilling that need within themselves to be actors and be actresses. It is not a place for, "Gee, I don't know what to do with my Wednesday mornings," or "I want to open up emotionally." For the students that I talk with and I sense would benefit and would contribute to our class, I invite them to do a working audit. The purpose of the working audit is for them to get a sense of how I teach and who I am and what I teach, and then also to participate so they will know by their own experience. And in this audit, by making certain adjustments in what the individual does, I can get a very clear clue as to whether they tune into this particular approach to acting. Some actors do not, because they need a very specific western logical structure.

Actors must come to believe in themselves and connect with their own power as human beings, with their own truth. And they need to know that not all of us are going to be accepting Academy Awards. Not all of us are even going to be able to earn enough in order to qualify for our SAG insurance. That cannot be the criteria for being an actor. We do it because we need to do it, and if you're only sense of success is the fame and money, you will never ever be happy. So, it's accepting yourself and it's accepting what life hands to you and using that well.

The Students of Jackie Benton

KATIE SHUFF

Working with Jackie, I am learning to let go of inhibitions and outside distractions and to focus my attention on my creative center. I have become natural and truthful as I have begun to allow the character to be revealed through taking risks and being vulnerable. I now trust myself and my abilities.

Jackie is compassionate, patient, professional and nurturing. I know that she truly cares about my thoughts and my feelings. With her guidance I have become the person and the actor I am today.

MARSHA ANN ROMANOFF

Some of the most important things I am learning from Jackie are: to come from my truth, to remove thought and to focus on the task at hand, to be centered, and to stop trying to "act." I have also learned how hard it is to truly surrender to the process and let go of expectations, to let go of results. And I trust Jackie. She is my teacher, my coach and my friend.

JEFFREY WEISSMAN

I have learned so many things from Jackie. I have learned to trust my instincts, to be in the moment, to understand the flow and rhythm of the script, and that as I evolve in my life—I evolve in my acting.

Every class is exciting and challenging. Jackie has been my spiritual guide and my compassionate advisor. If you are sensitive and want to grow, she is the best.

Jackie Benton: The Facts

Jackie Benton Studio
Santa Monica and Hollywood Locations
310-393-1410

Length of time teaching: over 30 years
Classes:
   Acting for Film and Cold reading
   Wednesday   10:00AM – 1:00PM
   Saturday   9:00AM – 12:00PM
   Scene Lab (as needed)
Private Coaching: $75 per 1 1/2 hours (minimum time)
Admission: Phone interview and working audit

Chapter 6
MICHAEL BOFSHEVER

I began to study acting in 1970 at Boston University School of Fine Arts, and interestingly enough, Michael Howard turned out to be my very first acting teacher. When I graduated college, having just done RICHARD THE THIRD with Al Pacino at the Theater Company of Boston and a year of summer stock at Tuft's Arena Theater as an actor, I moved to New York. An actress that had come up to Boston said, "Michael's teaching in New York now," and so I started to study with him in the fall of 1973 and have studied with him ever since that. I also had been an observer and an actor at the Actor's Studio for several years where I had the opportunity to sit in on classes with Lee Strasberg, Ellen Burstyn, Eli Wallach and Harvey Keitel. But Michael Howard by far is the most influential person as an actor for me. He taught me how to use all of myself in my work, and that what I had to offer was special and unique. I began to absorb Michaels love of actors, his love of the work and that the process is the most important and most exciting part of acting. The ways to create, the ways to use your instrument, to be like a sponge and to be pliable like clay, to use your child self—all of those things are things that I began to learn from Michael.

Class is a place to develop a process of how to work. We look to be able to bring out more than just the tip of the iceberg; we look to go beneath the surface with the actor to be able to touch different aspects of who they are. People need to know that they have a safe place to work and to be opening themselves up. We also work with learning how to relax, to physically let go of the tension and the things that are preventing us from being in touch with our entire instrument. We spend a lot of time learning how to let go of muscular tension through breathing exercises and through making sound. We then do different exercises so that the actor is expanding their creative imagination.

One of the things that happens for actors, especially in California, is that the business out there demands very little of your instrument. They look to place you in a certain category because of type or look and it's very hard to expand out of that. But most people who are really wanting to become artists are not getting into acting solely to make as much money as they can—there is a creative drive inside of them. Actors need to act. They need to have a place to expand their emotional energy that's underneath the surface. Otherwise, in a certain way, it's hard for them to breathe. And so we look to have a place where you can express that creative part of yourself and be in touch with all the different aspects of who you truly are. So when you go to an audition or you're working with a director, you will be able to touch this actor muscle that you have developed and worked on. Also, class is the place to get past the critic in your head that limits you and to get back to the joy of the work. The real world can really beat you down as an actor because of the enormous obstacles and constant negative feedback and rejection that actors get. And they need a place to replenish the well so that they can continue the spirit of why they became an actor in the first place.

I look to deal with each actor as an individual so that their needs are are being met. When new students get into class, we do a first monologue where we get an opportunity to work right away. We do different exercises together and it's an exciting, sometimes terrifying experience for actors, no matter what level that they're at. For me, I am finding out how they're going about it, how intuitive they are, how process oriented they are, what teachers they've studied with in the past so that I begin to understand how they're thinking. From there, as we build a trust between the two of us and we come to a common agreement, we begin to say, "OK, this is where we are. Let's begin to grow this part of you." So I start to recommend characters and playwrights that will address what the actor's specific needs are.

Needless to say, most directors out there don't know how to work with actors. They give actors results and ideas, concepts of how they think it should be, but they don't talk to them in doable terms. If there is anything, three words to live by for an actor is that, "Acting is doing." And at any one moment, you as an actor can be doing something. So actors need to know how to solve acting problems out there in the real world so when a director gives them a direction that is very result oriented, they can say, "OK, I know how to do something about that so that I am not trying to give you an idea but I'm making it interesting and creative for myself."

I think my greatest strength as a teacher is that I love doing what I'm doing. I love watching other actors grow. I also have a wonderful ability to communicate in language that actors understand. And I have a great compassion, because I am an actor myself. I have compassion for the obstacles that are involved in understanding the craft, let alone trying to get work. I don't want a class of people who are just in acting class. I want actors out there working, and I look to encourage them to get out there, to take what they're getting here and to put it to use. I also have this wonderful ability to understand how people operate and to be able to get through all the bullshit so that I am able to help them get to do what needs to be done.

The environment in my class is nurturing and challenging. It needs to be nurturing, so that they trust what we're doing and they feel that it's safe for them to let down their guard. And over time, as they do that, and we know that we are both there for the same reason, then the challenge is for me to help them cut away from the stuff that they're holding onto. I find, especially with a lot of young actors who are recently out of college or have been training just a little bit but were very successful in dinner theater some place, that they have a lot invested in bad acting. It may be fine someplace else, but for the most part, it's very superficial and not about them. And little by little, the student must begin to realize that the scene is about what they really know about it, not some idea that they got from a book or how it may sound to them. And that's challenging. You know, there seems to be for almost every actor in class a moment when they're going to have to really do the work, or then they end up finding reasons that they don't want to be in class. I know I had that moment for myself twenty-five years ago in Michael's class and I never forgot it.

The Students of Michael Bofshever

JILLIAN CRANE

Michael has taught me that I have a great resource of life to bring to my work. I have learned to trust myself more and to judge myself less. I have learned a way to get ready to work and I have found that I am becoming more and more a channel for artistic expression. I have also learned the importance of concentration and relaxation; two small words which hold the key to good work.

Michael is a working actor with a family and yet no matter what a student needs to talk about, he is there to be called or have a private meeting.

Michael urges us to be gentle with ourselves and our instrument. He has encouraged me to believe in myself and in my life and work.

FRANCIS SOLOMITA

I have acquired so many new tools in Michaels class. From how to work on "place" for a given scene and exploring dreams, to physically recreating through sense memory exercises. His class is about asking questions and I have discovered that not knowing the answers is the most dangerous and exciting place to be.

There is an understanding among the students in our class that this is a haven for experimenting and exploring—not performance. That class is not about doing a "good scene." What is important is learning and creating unique and imaginative avenues to solving material. Michael's class is challenging and stimulating if you are willing to take the journey.

LUCK HARI

I have learned from Michael how to find myself in the work—how to let the kernel of creativity begin with who I am, rather than with what my "ideas" are about the "character." I've experienced finding the role in my body rather than in my head and have had the exciting event during a scene when the burden of language was lifted; when it was no longer about speaking the text well

Michael creates the safest environment for exploration I've ever experienced. There is no "right" or "wrong"—there is only growth. I trust him implicitly. He works with each actor based on that actor's strengths, weaknesses and insecurities. He has a caring for each student that is individual, yet he has no "favorites"—rather, we are all his favorites. Michaels accessibility as a teacher is unmatched. And, as caring as he is, he constantly challenges us—it is discipline tempered with kindness.

Michael Bofshever: The Facts

Charles Conrad Studio
3rd Street Promenade
Santa Monica, CA 90401
310-281-9580
310-394-6133 (fax)

Length of time teaching: 10 years
Classes:
    Monday   6:30PM – 10:30PM
    Wednesday   6:30PM – 10:30PM
Private Coaching: Fee based on student's ability to pay
Admission: By interview

Chapter 7
GENE BUA

I hated school; I hated all aspects of school; I was terrified of school. I remember when I was in first grade, bringing home a report card with the highest grades in the class, and my father telling me, "Don't worry, you'll do better next time." And I knew that there was no way, I already was the best one in class, what did he want from me? I went to a very oppressive Catholic school and it was violent, and I tried not to go as often as possible. I wanted to sing, that's what I was going to be, a singer. And I did that. I was a rock and roll singer and I had a bunch of recordings and all of that. But at about twenty or twenty-one, a manager approached me and said, "You're good looking and you sing good. You should be an actor." I never even thought about being an actor, and I said, "But I don't know how to act." He said, "Oh, that doesn't make any difference, lots of people don't know how to act. I'll bring you to some director." So he brought me to Mordechai Lawner who directed me in a scene from GOLDEN BOY to do for a casting agent. And once in a while it would feel wonderful, but most of the time, it was awful. And I knew that there was something there that was more than me; that was bigger than me. So I started taking classes at the Neighborhood Playhouse in the evenings and I became absolutely determined that I was going to learn this art of acting, whatever the hell it was, and I was going to be able to do it well.

I remained in class for a long time, but soon after that I got a starring role on *Love of Life*, which was my first real break in television and I became quite a big day-time star. Other actors on the show would look at my work and they would say, "Wow, gee, what'd you do there? How do you do that?" And I would give them little hints and adjustments and in a sense, I became a teacher. I thought it was very important to have a real specific technique. And when I first started working in the show, I would sit down and spend hours on the script—I subtexted everything, I put the actions in and I decided how I wanted to do the emotional preparation. As the show progressed however, I began to need less time to work on things. All of a sudden, things began to happen that were more interesting and more fun than when I had worked it out. I was beginning to let go of the choices and I was discovering something greater than my mind. I remember doing a scene on my next show, *Another World Sommerset*, where I was working with Jo Beth Williams and she said, "But we haven't worked it out. What are we going to do? They're going to shoot it now." And I said, "Let's not work it out at all. Let's just do it. Let's just be present with each other in the moment and let's see what happens." And we did. This led me to start an acting class of day-time television stars; they all came over to my house after work and studied with me. And when I moved to L.A., I started a class and I invited in four students for free and if they liked it, to come back the next week and pay me and bring more people, and that's basically how I started.

I believe that there is a talent and that the talent knows. The more I try and make it be something that I think it should be, the less true it becomes. I believe that the marriage of your energy in the moment with the energy that's on that page, will spontaneously create a character. Many times, even a fully physical character that lives inside you. All I try to do is help each person find that place that knows; so we start by saying, "I don't know. I don't know what's going to happen." I start with the reading process because most of the time in the business, it's "Oh, hello, Gene. Come on in, we're running a little late. Just kind of look through this and let us know when you're ready. You ready, Gene? OK, go." There is an anxiety in that. There's an anxiety of "Oh my God, I got to do it right now. Oh my God, I've read it once. I don't know exactly what's going to happen. I can't sit down and sensorily go through every moment and I can't make three billion choices." So you have to be able to be spontaneous and in-the-moment. But most people try and do it the other way anyway. They try and read the lines a certain way, they try to make it be a certain something. And what I suggest when people first come in, in terms of cold reading, is that they don't try and make it anything. But that they explore what's really going on as opposed to what they think the scene should be about.

Recently, I thought, "You know, it would be cool to allow more choice back into the work. Now that you've thrown it away for so long, bring some more choice back." And this is how I do it—first, break down the scene into three pieces, three beats. Then, let's get to an action verb, but not an action verb like a lot of people teach them. How about for the first beat, a verb that says to investigate. To investigate what? If she's paying attention to me, investigate her sexuality, her soul, her eyes, the depth of her being, what she lives for—I mean, to investigate anything that in some way enlivens you, that interests you. The question then comes, well is that the right choice? Who the hell knows whether it's the right choice or not? And who cares! OK, now let's go to the second beat. What should we do there? How about to give a special gift of something. Of what? Of my undying affection or of my interest for her. In the third beat, let's reverse the special gift. Now this time, I'll take the special gift. And everything that the actor says has a different jolt to it, a different feeling because it's coming from them. When you leave it alone, it's like throwing the pebble into the lake and letting a rippling effect happen inside of you.

I also work with techniques that are more internal, and sensory related, as well as with music and with colors. To me, you can create with anything. Sometimes, I'll have students just open their pocketbooks or their wallets and put stuff on the floor and I'll say, "Pick up an object and that's what you're going to work from today." And then a wonderful story will come to them and it will come out in a fully emotional package.

I interview new people on the phone. And then if I get a good sense from them and they get the sense that they're interested, I have them come on in and take a class and pay for it. It's $46.25 and you put your money down. So we try it and at the end of class, we decide whether we want to work together or not. If we do, we commit for a month. I find that better than setting a day aside to do a whole bunch of interviews and look at people's pictures and all of that. I'm not interested in any of that anyway. I'm interested in what they're able to do when I work with them. So, I don't really care whether they've done anything or not. Matter of fact, much of the time, I prefer that they haven't. To tell you the absolute truth, the worst thing for me is somebody who comes in and thinks they know everything about everything, because they're very loathe to let go of what they think is correct and for these people, nothing new will ever happen.

My students all tell me that my class is the only place they've ever been where they feel that everybody there wants them to do well. It can be a real spiritual kind of experience. The trick then is for the student to bring that sense of daring-do to the marketplace where there isn't that same sense of support. I say to them, "There may not be, but you're also projecting that they know better than you when you walk in. The fact is that they don't.

They don't know what the right thing is. They perhaps know it when they see it." I once asked a casting director who came to class, "What do you look for?" She said, "we're so sick and bored of seeing the same goddamn thing coming in, one person after another after another. We look for somebody that has some sort of spontaneity or some sort of difference."

I love actors. Still. As long as I continue to create as a director or as a performer, and have my own creative life outside of the classroom, I think I will continue to love teaching actors. I've also learned over the years, that it's not about me getting my students to do every ounce that I think is in that material. It's about them doing it and eventually, that they don't do it for the teacher, they do it for themselves. And you know, as a teacher, I get to watch something happen that I don't understand—which is talent creating something. I see one person come together with one life and a whole point of view, and another person coming from another place, and the two of them letting go momentarily of their ideas and judgments of what they think things are—and then we get the third possibilities, the ones being created between the two of them, which are so much greater than either one of them could possibly have envisioned by themselves. And that's what hooks me on the goddamn process.

The Students of Gene Bua

KIM SWARTZ

I have learned from Mr. Bua that the most important tools for acting are already inside me, I just need to work through the things that distance myself from them, such as defenses, preconceptions and being too mental. Along with that I have learned to trust my own inner talent, to rely on it more, and to not force "untrue" or mere intellectually contrived aspects on my work. One of the most exciting moments for me was the first time I played a character who was a really disgusting person, a real jerk. I didn't see how I could do or say those things with any conviction or reality, but putting my trust in what I had been taught, it turned out to be the best work I had done up to that point. The hissing and booing from the female students was especially gratifying.

Mr. Bua is always open and responsive to any questions, comments and requests. It is possibly in identifying and working with needs that even we are not aware of that Mr. Bua excels. I am amazed at how caring and sensitive Mr. Bua is to the needs and feelings of each student. Working with him has not only improved my acting, but has helped me immeasurably in my personal and professional life.

TRACEY BREGMAN RECHT

What I find most amazing in Gene's class is watching the new actors perform. The first impression is that they should keep their day job. However within months, sometimes sooner, they are blowing you away on stage. My own growth has been exciting and rewarding. Friends, family and especially my producers have noticed a difference in my work since studying with Gene.

I have worked with many teachers and none of them have the energy and enthusiasm of Gene. His classes are filled with love, support and a tremendous knowledge of what he teaches. There has never been a time when Gene has not been there for me personally or professionally. After ten years, his support continues to warm my heart.

TONY HUSTON

Gene's attention to his students is absolute. I have never encountered a greater degree of concentration, such acuity when it comes to details of performance. He is also extremely sensitive to the vulnerable side of those in his care—I have never seen him expose a student to even the slightest embarrassment, let alone ridicule. His total concern is to help us to develop, to flower at our own rate. This does not mean that he cannot become irritated however—but only when the student is insincere, cheating himself in some way. Gene is very conscious that we are taking class to learn—he makes sure that we get our money's worth. Gene's teaching has permeated my whole life, I feel profoundly enriched and fortunate to have found him.

Gene Bua: The Facts

Gene Bua Acting For Life Theater
3435 West Magnolia Blvd.
Burbank, CA 91505
818-547-3810
818-547-3268

Length of time teaching: 20 years
Classes: From cold readings to completed scenes. All levels.
  (All classes approximately three hours long.)

Monday	6:00PM
Wednesday	10:00AM
Thursday	5:00PM
Friday	10:00AM

Private Coaching: $60 per half hour; $100 per hour
Admission: By phone interview and taking one class. (Fee for this single class is $46.25. After class Gene and student mutually decide yes or no.)

Chapter 8
RON BURRUS

I trained at the Stella Adler Conservatory in New York. Her teaching made sense to me, it kept the actor human, and I liked that. I was an ambitious, impatient actor and I wanted to get out and work. So I worked and I saw I didn't know it as well as I thought, so I returned and studied more. And then I went out and I worked for about five years and I made a choice as a young actor that the kind of work I was doing, I didn't care for. So I chose to teach, and Stella apprenticed me as a technique teacher and I worked with her in technique classes for ten years. After that, in 1984, I opened my own studio here in L.A.

The beginning work deals with how a person looks at life. The young actor starts to realize, "Oh my God, I'm acting in my life, but my life is not a play. It's not something I repeat over and over and over. So, I'm going to stop the acting in life and use it for my work." They also start to learn about basic communication, really relating to someone else. They see through the work that whatever choice you make in life, you're going to pay a price. Life is not this hunky-dory Disneyland all of the time. And acting forces you to look at the pain of living, use it and then move on.

I start with language from the point of view of getting the young actor to understand that words have an enormous power. It all starts with what are you talking about and what do you mean by what you say? This gets them into themes: what is love, what is revenge, what is greed? They are going to be playing material that is based on these large themes and these words have to have meaning for them. These words also have movement in them, which you're going to be using down the road when you start phrasing what you want, what you're doing and what your action is. I also start very early on with the imagination since that is the major building block of the technique. I don't go to the actor's personal life as the basis for the part, I go to their imagination—which contains their personal life. We also start to look at how to be physically comfortable in the circumstances; what are you doing there from the physical point of view and how are you living there without talking? Then we will start working on the structure of how to get to an action, what you want, what are you doing to get it, what's in your way, and the why—the justification, which I say is where your talent really is.

Stella's script interpretation was her greatest contribution to the field of technique for actors, that and character work. Now that's much later in the work for me, script and then character. There's the outside form of the character where you add the way the character speaks and any physical mannerisms. And then there's the inside, starting to realize what the difference is between you and the character. Now, how do you get on to the character's side? Because many times, you'll be working with actors for the longest time and they push, they indicate and eventually it slips out and they'll say, " You know, I never really liked this person." When you judge the character and what they do, you put a wall up between you and the character and who they are never really connects within you. Let the critics do the judgment, the actors job is to understand. So then there's a whole series of questions and answers in building a background for a character which leads you to understand why they are that way. In the very beginning of the work, I do an exercise called, "I want your life in five minutes." I use it not because I'm interested in your life personally, but I want the students to realize eventually, this is where character comes from. That you did not appear overnight—where and how you were raised influences you; certain high points and low points in your life took you in a certain direction, and now you've ended up here. It's the same thing with a character—they didn't come out of the blue. And when actors don't do this probing and imaginative work, there's no weight behind them. I work a lot for camera now, so when there's no weight behind them, the camera looks right at you and you're as empty as they come. You know, about eighty-five per cent of dialogue is coming from the past and if you haven't had the personal experience of the past, then it's empty, because you have no relationship to what you're talking about, let alone who you're talking to.

I only interview beginning actors because I don't expect them to know anything. But with more advanced actors who have trained differently and in other places, it's an interview and an audition. I'm interested in finding out if they have really enjoyed what they've done so far in acting, not that they were successful, but they enjoyed doing it. I'm also looking to see if they have the time, the energy and the need to learn. Sometimes they come with the value of "I want to be successful," or, "I just want to be popular." But if they stay in it, they come to respect the work that they do, and in turn, they respect themselves. My classes are disciplined and the students respect for each other, as partners in the work, is established early on. I'm very concerned about them realizing that actors have to be in a state of learning all the time, because they're responsible for understanding relationship—relationship to themselves and their relationship to the world. And relationship is always moving and changing, so you have to be very awake to keep up with yourself. Every time I see my students, my first two questions are, "What did you learn about life or acting or yourself from the last time I saw you?" and "What did you see specifically in life that held your attention visually?" So they start being aware consciously of where their talent lies. I know that I have a tendency to attract very independent thinkers who have a way of thinking for themselves, which I like since I don't consider myself an authority figure in teaching. I feel that I'm here to guide my students. I can't open the door, but I can guide them to the door.

The Students of Ron Burrus

DENISE VALLIN

I have learned from Ron the importance of making specific choices and how to personalize them, how to use my physicality and that I better believe in what I'm doing, because if I don't—no one else will. Ron doesn't "pass or fail" you in a scene, he gives you the opportunity to see your own mistakes and your own victories. I have also come to relax in my work and to not judge myself.

Ron doesn't cut the actor down to build that person into a "real" actor and he doesn't dance on the table when you finally understand something. To be his student and to learn from him, you must be self-motivated. Ron loves acting and loves teaching. He has given me incredible confidence in my craft and has allowed me to say, "I am a working actress!"

LAURA LEYVA

Some of the major things I have learned from Ron are: the use of my imagination, focusing my attention, looking for actions and understanding the theme of the material. He has given me the tools to lift the words off of the page and translate them into living form. This has been transformational for me.

Ron is always available to discuss new material, critique a performance, work on an audition piece or talk about life. He's there 100%. Ron's way of teaching is not just a path to a superior acting craft, it is a way of living life as an actor that is without doubt, pain or confusion. I have found Ron's work to be the most creative and life affirming process that I have ever experienced.

Ron Burrus: The Facts

Ron Burrus Acting Conservatory
Los Feliz Playhouse
4646 Hollywood Blvd.
Los Angeles, CA 90027
213-953-2823

Length of time teaching: 22 years
Classes: Call for specific schedule.
    Level I: Acting Foundation
    Level II: Scenes/Monologues and Cold Reading
    Level III: Script Interpretation/Character
    Level III: Rehearsal/Showcase Performance
Private Coaching: $75 per hour; $125 per hour (on the set)
Admission: Beginning actors: by interview. Advanced actors: by interview and audition.

Chapter 9
SANDRA CARUSO

After studying for a year at Boston University with David Pressman, I went to the Neighborhood Playhouse and studied with Sandy Meisner. I've had a lot of great teachers since him, but Sandy's was the training that stuck with me the most because there were definite tools that I could use. I studied with Uta Hagen at HB Studios, and what I loved about her was that she seemed to like me. She laughed when I performed, I mean in a nice way. She had a wonderful belly laugh and she was so with you as a student. She gave 100% of herself—emotionally and spiritually. Then I went to study with Lee Strasberg at the Strasberg Institute in New York City and my major memory about Lee was what happened when I had my interview with him. I had just come back from Europe where I had traveled for almost five months by myself and I had been quite lonely. I was very excited about this class, and I cried through the entire interview. I never stopped crying. I just kept apologizing profusely and he said to me, "It just means you're alive." I never forgot that; it was one of the greatest gifts a human being ever gave me, because he gave me permission to have my feelings and I carry that with me all the time. I started class the next day and I was in the same class as Marilyn Monroe and Jane Fonda, and my main acting partner was Gene Wilder, and so those were very good experiences. I found Lee's techniques difficult to grasp and hold onto. I thought he was a fascinating man and I could listen to him forever, but the actual tools that I use, I got from Sandy. And Sandy's influence is what led me to write my book, *The Actor's Book of Improvisation*.

Every student is highly individual. And I bring in a lot of different techniques based on what the student needs at the moment. I sometimes will bring in Michael Chekhov's approach when we need to physicalize and find the emotions that way—especially for some of the classically trained actors who have a slick facade that is very hard to break through. And I keep bringing my students back to the basics; I listen carefully and see if it's really happening between them, or are they just talking at each other. I will keep stopping them and giving them whatever exercise is needed at the moment to get them back on track. I also use a lot of the other arts in my acting classes. I bring in music and painting because I believe that actors need to be involved with and integrate all of the arts.

One thing that I work with a lot is the objective and the objectives opposite. I give the partners an improvisation with objectives; I have them make contact as they say what their objective is over and over to each other in a succinct sentence. But they will usually go for the fancy intellectual objectives. Oh, they'll say things like, "I want your respect." But that's in the head, that's intellectual. So I work very hard to get it out of the head and get it to something basic like, "I want you to rescue me." And then I always make them state the opposite of what they want. For example, "I want you to push me out into the world," or, "I want you to make me do this by myself," or, "I want you to make me feel terrible." You see, the opposite is always working in us. No matter what we want, there's always something pulling us in the other direction. Now, of course, I stress Sandy's point of "Don't do or say anything until the other person does or says something to make you do it." If they don't seem to be communicating, I will stop and have them state their objectives again and then go back into the improvisation. Then I will bring in the text and I'll have them do the same thing with the text, and the minute it sounds like they've lost connection, I stop them. I make them state the unspoken dialogue, what's really going on, improvise for a while, and then go back to the text until the text itself becomes an improvisation. Not that they are changing the words, but that they are personally experiencing the situation so it's them in those circumstances.

I also have students bring in a piece of music that makes them feel the way the character feels in the situation, and then I have them physicalize the way the music feels. That seems to take a lot of the self-consciousness and the tension away. They also bring in paintings that capture the essence of the person—sometimes they're portraits, sometimes it's an abstract painting that just gives the quality. If it's a portrait, they'll take the pose of the person, the dress of the person, get the facial expression of the person, and then go into the improvisation from that pose. A lot of interesting things come out of that.

I don't really consider myself a charismatic teacher, a big personality teacher. I think that my strengths are that I watch very carefully, and I deal with each student very individually. And because I've been teaching for so long, I feel as though I've gotten sharp at finding out what they need in the moment. I'm always studying and I have a terrific thirst for learning—I'm always going to conferences and taking other people's workshops. Also, I believe in sharing myself with the students, not just being this separate authority figure. I don't keep myself on a pedestal or separate from them. It's like we're working through this together and I'm willing to share some of my fears and vulnerabilities with them, which is something that I had liked in Uta Hagen. We are working with an art form and there's no point in trying to play any games because it's all about being human.

The Students of Sandra Caruso

JENNIFER SETTLOW

Sandra's emphasis is on my investing in creating a complete life for the character. Her focus on exploring the reasons behind each behavioral choice has led me to more fully inhabit each character I play and has taken my acting to new depths. I find that now my emotions flow more naturally and I am open to a heightened and freer experience.

Sandra is available, patient, very open and personal. She never dictates or preaches. Her style is nurturing and down to earth. Sandra goes out of her way to work outside of class with her students and she is gifted at helping us achieve a new awareness of our own acting abilities.

TESSA ZUGMEYER

In working with Sandra, I have gained a new freedom in the use of my own imagination. Out of this, I have experienced the magic of the text and a release of the emotions under the words. I have also learned the importance of specificity in my preparations to work. Being specific allows me to truly enter into the character's personal reality.

Sandra is a very supportive teacher who genuinely cares. Her classroom is always a safe environment to explore new ideas and to take risks. Sandra is always ready with constructive criticism and praises, and I know she is concerned about me—about my fears and my needs.

Sandra Caruso: The Facts

School of Theatre, Film and Television
UCLA
102 East Melnitz
Los Angeles, CA 90095-1622
310-476-5113

Length of time teaching: 25 years
Classes: Call for specific schedule
Private Coaching: $35 per hour
Admission: By audition and interview (For class but not for private
coaching)

Chapter 10
CAROLE D'ANDREA

My first class was when I was seventeen and it was at the American Academy of Dramatic Arts. After a year there, I went to Stella Adler and I studied with her for about two years. After that, I started working in my first show on Broadway, WEST SIDE STORY, and during that time I also started working with Lee Strasberg. Stella had so much to offer as far as intentions, condition, need and tension, that was her thrust—we didn't spend two hours trying to find a feeling. Lee did just the opposite. He was very adamant about going into your past life in finding those right moments. But I studied with so many wonderful teachers in New York—Warren Robertson, Elizabeth Palmer; I got so much from each of my teachers.

The fact is that we are always feeling something, especially when you walk into an audition or you walk into a performance. Your sensitivity is very high and very acute; you're hearing, you're seeing, you're smelling—everything is there. And what happens is most people leave ninety percent of themselves in the hall. They come in for the audition or the interview or the class and they leave ninety percent of their humanity outside. So, my philosophy is that first you have to create a safe environment, which the student respects and is committed to. You know, when somebody asked Michaelangelo how he sculpted David, he said, "I just chipped away everything that wasn't David." And that's what I think students are doing in class. So they have to have a trusting relationship with the teacher. And my approach is really about first getting the student comfortable with their own human condition. I always say, "Where are you right now? Is your heart open to this experience right now?" I work with the senses, with sense memory and with the students creative imagination. That's what I think we draw on in life. We only have our own experience and our imagination. I'm also very big about being in-the-moment, reacting and really listening. It's so critical to get the student to be in the now.

If it's scene week, the first thing I have them ask as they look at the text is, what is the character feeling. That's the condition. Then, what is the need of the character, what is the overall objective. And then, what are the intentions? Stella called them actions, Uta Hagen called them intentions—it makes no difference. What are you doing to get your need met in this scene? That's basic and that's what I start with in every scene. And then we talk about the preparation: where did you just come from, what's going on and most importantly, how do you identify with this event and with this character? For example, if I were doing MARY, QUEEN OF SCOTS and I was playing Mary, the first thing I would ask is, "When did I feel threatened in my own life? When did I feel that the stakes were so high that I had to fight for my very existence and my validation?" And then I would allow those images to come up for me. I always talk about letting the images come up, because we take pictures our entire lives; we have so many images in us. It's like pushing a little button. You say, "Oh my gosh. There it is. I know exactly when I felt that way."

You know, everything in acting is sort of conflicting. I spend a lot of time saying don't zero in on the words but I'll give you an example of how important I think words are. I've developed an exercise about two months ago that I use in my classes that has been really wonderful. You take a line of text and see where the key word is. The student will take a line from their monologue or their scene and they would say it to their partner. Let's say the line is, "I called my mother and she was furious at me." And I have them emphasize the first word. "*I* called my mother and she was furious at me." Then I have them emphasize the second word, " I *called* my mother and she was furious at me." We go through the whole line this way to see what the key word is and each time they do it, their partner responds to what they are getting as the character. The students have found this exercise very useful. So I am really doing a great variety of kinds of approaches to the work with my students—always leading them to make wonderful and specific personal choices. When we're specific, that's when the feeling comes, just like in real life.

I think I'm a very nurturing teacher. I have great respect for the sensibilities, feelings and individual process of every student. I never take somebody where I don't think they're ready to go. I know that the students I work with say, "I can't wait to get to class to see what you're going to do next, Carole. It is so much fun in there." That makes me so happy because that's how I feel. A lot of teachers get locked into a specific technique and it drones on and on, month after month after month. It's like, "OK, we smelled the coffee for two months now. Can we move on?" So I love to shake the students up, just throw them a curve and start in a whole different direction. Also, I always encourage students to write their own material if they feel that they have even an iota of an urge towards that. As a result, my God, my students are doing one man shows, they're writing music, and I'm very moved by that.

You know I started in musical theater and I teach a singing performance class on Tuesdays, which I've been teaching for the past sixteen years. I teach it just like my acting class because the song is the same as doing a monologue. You break everything down the same way. You see, music heightens all of our sensitivities, our awareness and our emotional life and it's why a lot of actors are a little scared of it. I have actors whisper in my ear all the time, "Carole, I've always wanted to sing and I'm a little frightened—I feel so exposed when I sing." But it's the most extraordinary situation to experience. To get into this class, students must come in and audit. There is a $20 audit fee and they can sing in class. Now, it's not mandatory, but I really suggest that they do sing. I tell them that it is not an audition but that it gives me a chance to see where they are. For the acting class, they audit two classes. They come and see one scene week, and they come and see one monologue week. Only after auditing can they set up an interview with me.

Over the years, I have learned painfully that the only way to have healthy classes and to attract responsible people is not to enable dropping in and dropping out; not to allow students to pay when they feel like it; not to allow students to be disrespectful of their classmates by leaving class early. It's not worth it for me to even start with anybody who says, "Oh, I can come in for two or three months." I mean, why bother; I don't even go there anymore. I do an hour interview with every student. I'm looking for integrity and a passion to learn, I'm looking for heart. And I will give all of my experience and all my excitement and my love of teaching to them, if they're willing to give themselves a chance and commit to a process that takes time. With great joy, I will help them bring to life their own, individual talent.

The Students of Carole D'Andrea

MELISSA JUSTIN

With Carole, there is never one right way to do something—and nothing is ever wrong if it works for you. She is so creative in her teaching methods and so I have benefited by having learned a lot of different techniques, possibilities and keys to achieving what I am trying to do. I think the emphasis of Carole's technique is self-reliance and the freedom of exploration. I am continually learning more about how to work with my body, mind and heart as an actress. In professional situations, I am now calm and I have the faith and freedom to be myself.

Carole is an enormously special person. Without ever imposing her beliefs, she shares with us her love, wisdom, generosity, intellect and great life experience. She has so enhanced and enriched my life, and she has given me a joy in pursuing my dreams.

HILARY MORSE

I was first attracted to Carole's class because I found that most of her students are working! Most importantly, I am learning from her how to trust my instincts; how to be simple, specific and honest. Carole's ability to see who I really am and her wisdom in the ways she has encouraged me to explore myself have been of great value.

Carole is gentle, supportive and available, and she has helped my talent flourish. I have experienced huge growth and witnessed it in my classmates. Carole nudges me into areas that I need to work on, and she always leaves me feeling like a winner.

Carole D'Andrea: The Facts

Flight Theatre
6472 Santa Monica Blvd.
Hollywood, CA
818-759-9416

Length of time teaching: 15 years
Classes: (Carole also teaches master classes in NYC in September.)
    Acting Classes
    Wednesday   11:30AM – 2:00PM
    Thursday   11:30AM – 2:00PM
    Singing Performance Class
    Tuesday   10:00AM – 2:00PM
Private Coaching: $75 per hour
Admission: By audit first and then interview

Chapter 11
WAYNE DVORAK

I started in community theater when I was 16, and did quite a few plays before I got into college. And then I was on scholarship at the University of Minnesota. Because they were just building the Guthrie Theater, people like Bobby Lewis, Arthur Miller and Guthrie were there. And being a theater major, we all benefited from their mentorship. But we never really learned a solid and specific technique, nothing that actually related to the actor's inner life and any emotional basis for scenes. Eventually, after getting a masters degree in theatre and studying here in L.A., I opened a studio of my own. I developed an acting program, and for my actors who I felt were ready to pursue connections, I brought in agents and casting directors to take a look at these kids. One day, a casting director named Jane Feinberg came in and took a look at the work and she said, "You know, there's only one or two people I could bring in and the rest of them are not what I need. Their acting is not what I could bring in for film auditions." And I said, "Well, what do you think the major problem is?" And she said, "Well, you know, I can give them a script and in minutes they can get it practically memorized, make choices and get up there and perform it, and dah, dah, dah—but it's not very real and it's not based in them emotionally." She said that they needed to do more organic work in their training. I had reservations with some of the organic kinds of exercises that I had done and seen happen in classes. I found that the teacher could get the students into deep emotional things based on their own personal lives and their own scar tissue, but not able to get them out of it. And I felt that that was just too psychologically damaging to the actor and I didn't want to take that on.

I was aware of the approach developed by Sanford Meisner and I knew an actor who had worked with Sandy in New York and was teaching, so I brought him in to work with my students. Within three months of them doing exercise work, in seeing their tape work, (because some of the exercises were taped,) I noticed that they were connecting emotionally and becoming more emotionally truthful. I was very impressed with that and I decided to do the training myself. Now, I offer this work in a two-year format at my studio and to me, it is the best foundation for an actor; one that will produce a healthy actor who can approach his work from an emotional point of view and from an artistic point of view without doing any psychic damage. Which is very important to me because I really believe that we're here to lead healthy, happy lives. And a lot of times actors feel that they must be tortured and tormented to be good and I don't think that proves to be true when you look at the major people actually working in film and on stage.

I always start with what I think the student needs to learn as an individual. A lot of it depends on how much training someone has when they come to me. I've trained people that have been on Broadway and that presents a certain kind of a problem, or I'll get people that have never studied before and that will present certain problems. I don't push actors, I think that can be very damaging. I just look at their work and tell them what I think that they were doing and what they need to do to improve it. Also, I keep my classes very small. There are between ten and twelve people in a class so that the actors do a lot of work—and I try not to talk too much. I will develop a comfort zone first between me and the actor and then as I start finding out how they're developing, I will suggest certain emotional areas that seem to be lacking. Let's say that they're very good at reaching pain. Well, maybe anger could be a block, or maybe their sexuality, or sometimes their sense of humor is lacking. So I'll have them work in certain areas so that they develop as an actor who is comfortable expressing just about anything.

In the first year, I try to find material that is based more on the relationship rather than the character, so that they can explore who they are in all these scenes and learn to deepen everything from their own point of view. Then, they get to the character work in the second year. And they'll work on the classics so they get a taste of what great writing is. Sometimes, I'll give them something which is not particularly well written, because the reality of it is that you don't always get a script that's great, especially in television—but your job is to make it come alive in a real way. I also stress the business part of acting at the studio. I developed a mentor program, working with a group called "Colors United," where a full scholarship is given to an inner-city kid. I also have professional directors, producers and writers come in and watch the development of the actors and there's a very free exchange of ideas and information from these mentors. Which is so valuable because actors have a tendency to believe that they are the only people that are struggling and having a hard time finding projects, and that simply isn't true.

I think my strengths are that I'm very patient, I'm relentless and I have a good background both academically and professionally. I've been acting professionally for about 20 years. Mostly television, some film work and I did a lot of stage work prior to coming to Hollywood. I'm still a working actor and I'm out there and I know what's going on. And I try to encourage my students to pursue their spirituality, whatever that means to them, because I think that's the real heart of the actor. I encourage my students to go to art museums, to read great literature and the great playwrights. I put artwork in my studio for my students to look at—I have African masks and statues, I have Mexican work and Southwestern, Eskimo works and American Indian. I recently bought a five child Buddha—when you look at it, you have to smile. The environment in my class is casual. Of course, there is no response when people are working, no laughing or any sounds, but in between, I feel that they should be talking and laughing and having a good time. I don't like to get too sanctimonious about it and I certainly don't like to add any kind of fear or depression to the situation. I try to keep it positive with a certain amount of humor.

New students come into class by an interview and an audit. I want to make sure that they're comfortable with the group and with me before anything is really decided. I'm always looking for people that are positive and serious about what they're doing. I try to discourage people who think that they're going to come in here and take six months of classes and go on television or film. And I do expect my students to work outside of class and to be prepared when they come in to show me their work, because that's all I'm correcting or giving them information on. I'm interested in developing people that are there to get as much from me as they possibly can get.

The Students of Wayne Dvorak

ERIC PRESCOTT

I am learning from Wayne how to simplify things, to connect emotionally to myself and to others, and to respond truthfully in each moment. I have felt a new freedom as I have started to release inhibitions, self-doubt and the blocks I have placed on myself to keep people from judging my behavior. I am now much looser and willing to take risks, which has been of great value in my work and in my day-to-day life.

Wayne is so available to us. He really listens and tries to help— whether we don't understand something or simply need advise on something or simply need advice on the logistics of doing a scene. You can always tell that Wayne is doing it because he really enjoys seeing the students' progress.

LORI EVANS

I have been studying with Wayne for seven months and most importantly, I am learning how to be free with my body and my emotions. I am now able to get out of my head (most of the time) and focus on my objective or my partner. I have been amazed by the range of emotions I have experienced and witnessed in my class.

Wayne is very patient and encourages us to move forward by taking risks. He never harasses anyone into doing something and he never puts anyone down. In his class, I feel safe to be vulnerable and yet I know that I am still in control.

TERRANCE C. JONES

I get a huge rush from the work I am doing in Wayne's class. It has been so exciting to create true intimacy with myself and my scene partner, and to allow myself the freedom to act on my feelings. I am now a more honest person which I know has made me a better person and a better actor. I am also learning from Wayne what it is to be a professional, both in my work and in the business side of acting.

Wayne is always very supportive. He's actually harped on me a couple of times for not calling him when I was unsure about an exercise I had to bring into class. He's also been very available to me during my quest for representation. Inside as well as outside of class, I know that Wayne really gives a damn about his students.

Wayne Dvorak: The Facts

Dvorak & Company
1949 Hillhurst Ave.
Los Angeles, CA 90027
213-462-5328

Length of time teaching: 20 years
Classes:

Professional Level: Monday   7:30PM
First-year Meisner: Wednesday   7:30PM
Second-year Meisner: Tuesday   7:30PM

Also, cold reading/audition class (call for specific schedule)
Private Coaching: $60 per hour
Admission: By interview (in some cases, new students must also audition)

Chapter 12

DAPHNE ECKLER-KIRBY

Although I had many other acting teachers in New York, Larry Moss is the one who I consider to be my mentor. He helped me lose my fears, get technically clean and really understand the process of acting. But I think the greatest gift he gave me was a very gentle, nurturing, supportive attitude while maintaining very high standards of work. When I moved out to Los Angeles in 1980, I started working professionally and didn't study until Larry moved out here—and then I joined his professional class. When I win my academy award, he's going to be the first one I thank.

When I started teaching, I looked deeply inside myself to see what helped me as an actor, because I think I was pretty typical in the sense that most actors have baggage from their childhood, judgments about expressing emotion and a lot of fear about being vulnerable. You know, acting felt very scary to me in the beginning. So I have great compassion in my teaching and a reverence for the art, and I use the techniques that I have found to be most productive.

Even though I'm known as someone who helps people master the auditioning process, my work isn't limited to that. When someone calls me up, I often have a private, hour and a half interview with them and we cold read together. We talk about the process of how they have learned to break down a script: do they work with intentions; what's their past training; what's worked for them? And I start working very gently and intimately with them to make more specific choices in the script. I like to work with intentions right away, which gets them to be active rather than passive. I'll then share with them what level I feel their work is at. And in this session, they can also see if they like the way that I work, and my energy.

The acting student and teacher relationship must be based on trust, for the actor must feel comfortable enough with the teacher to expose their most vulnerable areas—which are usually the areas of fear and anxiety. It is an essential ingredient for an artist's growth, because you're exploring human behavior and you're exploring your own process, your own psyche, your own emotions, sexuality and intellect. I adore actors. My class has a very supportive environment and what I try to do is build on and reinforce the actor's strengths. I consider myself a very honest teacher. So it's a delicate balance between pushing somebody to go forward and still supporting what they have.

My class is primarily about approaching the work for TV and film. So when the students come in, I give them a three or four page script based on their physicality and their type. They then have about 40 minutes to memorize the script, make their choices and practice it out loud. Then I start putting them on-camera as if this were the actual audition and I work with them to get the audition to the level of either a call-back or a booking. If the emotional condition is off, I will work with the actor emotionally; if the physicality of the character is off, we'll work on that; if the choices are non-specific, we work on coming up with different intentions and using their own life to call forth these experiences. So it's very individualized. I also try to simulate as much as possible the things that actors are faced with—the pressure of auditioning for the networks, or for producers. Out here in Los Angeles, it's really the whole package that they're buying, which is very uncomfortable for some actors to realize. And it's not always the best actor who gets the job.

I don't have very many real beginners in my class, I consider it more a professional class. If an actor is way below the work level of my class, I'll offer to teach them for several months privately until they get up to snuff. In my private coaching I work with people on preparing for specific auditions and I also work with people who are very fragile, who have a lot of fear and they're scared to go into a class. I think my strength is my personal knowledge of the business because I've been an actor for 24 years myself and I'm still a working actor. So I know what it requires to have a professional career. And the other thing I do, which I could have benefited from when I was a young actor, is career counseling. So the actors in my class are not only working on the art and mastering the craft of it, but I do everything from helping them write letters to agents, to submitting themselves, to counseling them about their pictures, to getting them very clear on how they're going to be cast and what their strongest suits are. I get them very aware of what I call their trump cards, which are their individual strengths as actors. I teach a class with very high motivation in the sense of going out there and making careers happen. I make goals with the actors and I usually have actors enthusiastically keep them. It's not me being a task master, but we sit down and make goals together in a very realistic game plan of getting the career going. And I'll even go as far as advising people that they're not dressing right, their personality's off or they need to do some work in therapy. I take on the whole person; I guide them and hold their hands because Los Angeles can be very scary and very frustrating.

I love the people that I have in my class and I love seeing them grow. I love seeing people get excited about the possibilities that they can create. Also, I teach with a lot of humor. I try to lighten the load, because I usually find a group of actors to be very anxious, frustrated, tense and very scared that their careers won't happen. So, we have a lot of humor, a lot of rapport and I can't think of any place that's more fun. Sometimes, when I've worked all day and I'm exhausted and I go, "Oh no, I have to teach tonight," all of a sudden the class is an hour over and I'm high as a kite and I can't sleep at the end of it.

The Students of Daphne Eckler-Kirby

NAN WOLFF

Working with Daphne, I now have a stronger passion for my creativity than ever before. She instills in us the ability to believe in ourselves; to be able to see in a tape playback just where we are in the learning process and what needs to be done to shape ourselves in order to give our best. Daphne's class is a place to create and to experiment and each week I leave class with the best "high" I've ever had in my life.

Daphne's nurturing spirit is one of the main things that keeps me going when everything else appears to be going poorly. I value her sternness in "riding me," because she knows I can do better work. I trust Daphne implicitly—in my book, she's an amazing teacher, an extraordinary human being and I can only give praise and thanks for what she's done for me.

THOMAS MILLS

With Daphne, I am learning how to better take the text and develop meaningful characterizations. I'm learning to trust my instincts and take chances rather than remaining safe. In Daphne's practical approach, there is no mumbo-jumbo; she teaches me how to make good choices so that when I walk into an audition, I am ready for action. Her class is no place to be whiny or bitter. Daphne knows that class and life should be about working hard and improving yourself; she teaches it—she lives it too.

This is the only time I have studied with someone where I felt growth every week. When you work with Daphne, you not only become a better performer, she builds your self-esteem. And on short notice, Daphne is always available to me. Simply put, I've improved my acting abilities and I certainly would never have sat down and written about any other acting teacher I've ever had.

Daphne Eckler-Kirby: The Facts

Call for location in Studio City
818-769-9709

Length of time teaching: 10 years.
Classes:
> *On-Camera Acting Workshop*
> Monday   12:00PM – 3:00PM
> Tuesday   7:00PM – 10:00PM

Private Coaching: $40 per half hour; $75 per hour
Admission: By telephone interview

Chapter 13
ALAN FEINSTEIN

I began in New York at the Dramatic Workshop, where I studied for two and a half years. I was then a pretty regular working actor when someone told me about a class they were in with a teacher named Warren Robertson. I ended up spending about six years with Warren. He felt that emotions have been stored away and locked inside the body by our life experience; that once we experienced these blocked emotions, they could then be put into our work. Which is actually the title of my own workshop, I call it "Emotion into Action." I found Warren to be a very sensitive and patient teacher. He helped me free my voice and my body and feel safe enough to have very big emotional breakthroughs. And it seems in retrospect that almost congruently, major things changed in my career, the pinnacle of which at the time is that I was hired by Tennessee Williams to play Stanley Kowalski in the 25th anniversary production of A Streetcar Named Desire on Broadway. There is no doubt in my mind that if eight months before these things didn't start to change, I could have never played that role. When I came out to LA, a friend of mine was studying with Milton Katselas and I decided to join his class. I stayed at Milton's for eleven and a half years, and it was Milton who got me into teaching. A lot of actors have said to me, "You're a working actor, you know how to act. Why are you in class?" I've spent something like 21 years in class, regardless of how successful my career was going. I would say, "Well, if I want to do a piece from ZORBA THE GREEK, I can do it in class, because if I wait until I'm hired to do this, it may never happen." Aside from the fact that it's fun and it's fun seeing other people doing things, changing, growing, trying and risking—it just seems very fundamental to me.

When I got into it in the early sixties, people would talk about, "Well I want to work hard enough and then audition for the Actor's Studio." Or,

"I want to be a terrific stage actor." And they were filling themselves up with knowledge of what had gone on ever since the Group Theater. When I mention the Group Theater to young students today, they don't have a clue. They don't even know of the Actor's Studio. I find that most students today are looking for a very fast fix. I get calls and they say, "Well, how long is your course?" And I go, "Well, what do you mean?" And they go, "Is it four weeks, six weeks or eight weeks, because I really want to get a TV series." And I'm just aghast, I don't even know what to say to them.

My heart goes out to everybody that's trying to do this and I try to come from a very supportive and encouraging place. I have sat in classes where teachers have berated their students, you know, "What kind of shit is this?" and, "You better get with it." And I have seen students that only feel that they're learning when they're being clobbered. But my own philosophy is to, in essence, point out what's good, encourage what needs work, and try to explain the difference with a "how-to" along with it. I try to incorporate whatever has been my life experience into the solution at the moment so that if someone's in my class long enough, they're going to be doing sensory work, they're going to be doing some of Meisner's work, they're going to be doing some of Warren's work, and they're going to be doing some of what my gut instinct says. I work with each student individually, so anyone watching is going to be picking up different information. It's a matter of spending a significant amount of time in my class to have it start to come together.

In terms of the emotional work, initially, I might have the student just standing on the stage, arms relaxed to the sides and I will give them some word stimulus. Then they see what comes out and leave it alone. Now, I might combine that with some of the things from a song and dance exercise, skipping around the room or adding some wild gyrations. And then when someone is in somewhat of an emotional state, let's say they're working that night on a monologue, then they do the monologue. For example, let's say someone is working on the last speech from I NEVER SANG FOR MY FATHER, where he says, "Death ends a relation for the life of that relationship." If someone were very bound up, I might give them an exercise in which they would say, "I love you, I miss you, don't go." And there's usually someone that they can relate those words to. They don't have to tell us who that is, they just need to know who it is. It might be them as a child being in their room alone, frightened at night, being put to bed, and a parent is walking out of the room, and they feel, "Don't go," and they have all this anxiety, fear of loss, etc. Then if any of that is touched and then they do the monologue again, it takes on a new and real and active life.

I think almost every actor, as youngsters at some level, we were emotionally invisible or felt that we were. That somehow our opinions and feelings were not recognized. And I think that is a big core of what's behind most people that want to perform. And teaching, helping people get past the restrictions of our social habits, seems to give me a juice, it stimulates me. I find that by the end of an evening, the students are falling asleep and I'm still going. When Milton first asked me to teach, I said, "What am I going to say? Oh my God, what if I have absolutely nothing to say?" That was my initial fear with the very first class, and if anything, now I find I have to watch myself, that I don't try to cover too much in one night. Teaching acting is very challenging and I care very much that I'm saying something that they're getting. I find that when the students are really doing the work, I see a difference in their self-esteem, and when they come to me and say, "Thank you for helping me," I feel just great. I think that the environment in my class is very supportive, with a certain amount of fun and humor. I think everyone that has stayed with me feels a sense of personal interest and care in them.

The Students of Alan Feinstein

VI DUPRE

Alan is very perceptive. He identifies your idiosyncratic ways of "hiding" and helps you identify them and work to overcome them—or to work with them rather than letting them overshadow your work. He has a way of encouraging you to grow, to expand, to search for the emotion and energy of a character who is real and believable. Alan has taught me preparedness, professionalism and commitment. He has also taught me how to take risks; that if I commit to my choice, even if it is wrong or not the direction that the director chooses to go, it presents me as an actor who has creativity and the ability to extend.

Alan has stressed that being an actor is an on-going process. That we must be aware and observant of every human experience. That we bring all that we are to our work. That there is always a need to study, to work, to practice our craft—to enrich and expand it. That being an actor of worth is not an intellectual accomplishment, but a human one.

A most exciting moment for me in Alan's class came when I was struggling with a scene. I was frustrated to the point that Alan asked my partner to get off the stage. I was left there with my feet firmly planted as Alan asked me to do a simple exercise that has since changed my life. It revealed to me the source of my problem—not that I could not act, but that there was rage, guilt and other hidden emotions that had been bottled up for so long. In this moment, I broke through a wall of emotions that were holding me back from my best work—as well as effecting my health.

Alan is one of the most professional people I know. He is always on time and he gives each class his absolute best. He always gives every student his undivided attention no matter what level he or she may be at. I know that whether it is to discuss scenes, auditions or personal issues, Alan is always there for me.

Alan Feinstein: The Facts

Lionstar Theater
12655 Ventura Blvd.
Studio City, CA 91604
213-650-7766

Length of time teaching: 10 years
Classes:
    Scene Study
    Monday   7:00PM – 11:00PM
    Cold Reading/Auditions
    Saturday   9:00AM – 12:45PM
Private Coaching: $60 per hour
Admission: By interview

Chapter 14
JANE HALLAREN

The teacher who was my major inspiration was Allan Miller. He was just marvelously creative and wonderfully exciting. I learned preparation from Allan, I learned freedom and I learned how to accept and look at almost everything around me as inspirational. Marilyn Freid was also a wonderful teacher for me. She brought me back to habituating the foundation of preparation, and in this particular case, it was the sensory work.

When I started teaching, one night I dreamt that I had a school and it was this big Victorian house and in the house was every acting method that had ever been taught. When I woke up I thought, "That's it. That's my philosophy. That's what I believe in." That there is no one method that works for everyone at all times, nor is there any method that should be sneered at. You can be trained as a sensory actor as I was, and then come across a part that you may plunge into every possible sensory and historically emotional situation of your life and come up dry—and then put on a costume and there it is. So, I guess if there's anything I'm against in the creative process, it's the person who says, "This" is the method. The methods themselves all have their place.

You know, we like to compare ourselves to the English and say, "Well, the English are external actors." I think English actors are wonderful. And then there are the Russians. They are like Marlon Brando: there's Brando and then there's everybody else. The Russians are so supreme because they are extraordinarily trained; they are just incredible in their physicality and vocal ability and dexterity. We don't address these things here. Not that we couldn't do it, but we're a nation based on commerce and so unsupported in the arts. So we go for the McDonalds' philosophy throughout—what can I learn the quickest way to get me to earn money? Now, this isn't what any artist really wants to do; they want to revel in their art, but we're forced a great deal of time to think of the money.

I believe strongly in teaching technique and preparation and that is what I do in the first part of my classes. I think it's major, major, major. The second part of my class is always given over to scenes and monologues, but only by working with the techniques that we're learning in the first part. For a young actor who has not yet established a technique, I see no value in just a scene study class. What for? So that he or she can get up in front of 20 people and the teacher can say, "You didn't do this and you didn't do that."? Well, tell them how to do that! I want my students to leave with a tool kit that is enormous so that they know how to work, how to experiment and explore.

I have exercises designed to keep the actor from performing their pre-conditioned ideas of how they think it should go. That concept and that particular philosophy came right from Allan Miller, who never left anything alone. "You got that? Boom, boom—change it. Boom, boom—change it. Boom, boom—change it." And not change for change sake, but change because we're changing all the time. You hear actors say, "Oh, it's so hard for me to make this shift." But we make transitions constantly in life. It's only our fear that says, "Oh, I can't make that transition." When kids play cowboys and Indians, they don't have any trouble transitioning from the cowboy into the Indian. They just change. I don't know any child who has trouble with that shift. In my recent trip to my mother's funeral, I heard the flight attendant say, "Please check your belongings. Things shift in flight." And I thought, "Ah-hah. And well they should!" That's what actors must do—shift in flight. And you never lose truth. You only lose truth when you're judging yourself and when you're thinking about what you're going to do next.

My major strength as a teacher is that I refuse to put blinders on myself or any of my students and I promise to guide them. Also, I love to teach and I love actors. I have a passion to get back to the classroom. I learn when I teach. And I have to shake it up and change all the time. I would love it if teachers went around and saw each other's classes and learned from one another. I don't have a big possessive deal; of course, that's also why I'm not business oriented in this job. I like small classes, never more than ten students at a time. I want to know and nurture each person because then I can help them better—and that's what's exciting to me. It bores me when there's a lot of people and I don't ever want to be bored. I want to be totally clear and focused. My other strength is that I've got a great eye. In my life before acting, I was a modeling agent. And the reason I was so successful was because of that eye. I just am gifted with a good eye and a good ear so that it's hard to bullshit me. But having said that, as a teacher, there's a great way of not saying, "That's bullshit." I believe in saying, "Ah, I know this problem. This is a good problem. I have exactly the same problem, and here's what I think we can do with it." Also, I'm not a priest and I'm not a shrink. So I never will say anything that's attached to any psychological methodology. There are no confessions in my class; I've seen that technique and I was appalled and frightened by it.

If you are in my class, you have to do certain things: you're obliged to be reading a good novel; you're obliged to go to a museum; you're obliged to see at least three movies or plays or dance a week and listen to classical music. So you get a lot of homework with me. You see, everything is a source of inspiration and the one major way of getting inspiration is the tedious discipline of working every single day. You cannot escape tedium. If you come into acting or any of the arts to escape having a nine-to-five job, you're making a mistake, because you gotta do the same thing people who have nine-to-five jobs do. You've got to go through the tedium of habituating working constantly, on your craft—and then inspiration comes.

The Students of Jane Hallaren

Nan Temkin Dudley

Jane has a basic structure in her class that is based upon her work with the method, but she is continually introducing new exercises and approaches to breaking down emotional barriers and solving problems. She is also a master at teaching improvisational exercises in which we are demanded to react and behave spontaneously. In my work with Jane, I have learned to value myself as a human being and to trust my talent and my instincts as an actress. I have also learned to get out of my own way and not to concern myself with what others might think about me.

Jane is always available to her students, supportive of their needs and interested in each person's unique situation. She is sympathetic and compassionate but doesn't allow people to take advantage of her. Jane teaches us to care and think for ourselves.

JOSEPH MALONE

I have had the opportunity to study with many teachers but no one has the practical approach that Jane offers. It is a technique designed to free actors of concept, focusing us on our emotional impulses and the expression of our truth in the moment. All of this while never allowing us to forget that the relationship with the other character in the scene is the crucial connection.

Jane has worked with me until I am clear and understand what I need to do to solve a particular acting problem, regardless of how long that may take. There have been numerous times I have called Jane from a movie or television set desperately seeking her help. She can always make sense out of some note I have gotten from a director who has offered me no concrete acting solutions. It would be no exaggeration to say that if I had not studied with Jane, it would be doubtful if I would have continued acting at all much less have a successful career. I am eternally grateful to her.

SHERRY LANE THOMAS

Jane has encouraged me to explore and follow all of my instincts; to trust myself. Jane has never told me what to do, she has guided me in such a way that I am able to do the work on my own. Whether I have months or minutes to prepare, I now have the tools and I know I will never be lost. Jane is positive, supportive and knowledgeable and has taken me to places I never thought possible.

Jane Hallaren: The Facts

1144 North Vista
Los Angeles, CA 90046
213-969-8089

Length of time teaching: 15 years
Classes: Ongoing classes (call for current schedule)
Private Coaching: $75 per hour (for a single session); $60 per hour (for a series of ten sessions)
Admission: By interview

Chapter 15
ADAM HILL

I originally started with Stella Adler and I completed my two-year course with her, but I always felt that I never quite got the full craft of acting; I always felt like there was something missing. I was very lucky to audition for and get into the ABA Repertory Company in New York, which was the only repertory company on Broadway at that time. While I was with them, we had to take classes everyday, and so we studied with a myriad of people. That's where I learned the Strasberg technique as well as Sanford Meisner's approach. But if you ask me who my mentor is, it would be Rosemary Harris. What she gave me was a love of and a respect for the craft. So it was not a specific acting tool, it was her whole persona, how she approached her work. I remember one day when she was doing LION IN WINTER, we were going out to have dinner together and I couldn't find her and they told me that she was on stage. When I looked, I couldn't see her and I finally said, "Rosemary, are you around?" And she popped up from in between the seats. She had been walking up the aisles and she noticed that there was some stuff left on the floor after the clean-up. And she was out there, the Tony award winning star of LION IN WINTER on Broadway, cleaning up the house as she said, "Just making sure it's clean for my audience."

I started teaching in the early '70s. Whenever I did a play, the other actors would always come to me for advice. I guess I had a little invisible sign around me that said, "Teacher," because everyone seemed to come to me that way. After one particular production, the actors in the company said, "Well, would you just get together with us and maybe have a few classes?" And I said, "I don't want to be a teacher. " And they said, "Oh come on, Adam, please, please, please." And I said, "OK, but just for a few weeks." And I've been doing it ever since.

My philosophy is very simple. There are the tools of acting and the actor has to find out which tools are going to work the best for them. I don't believe in any one of what I call "the gurus," I believe in all of them. And I believe every single one of them had a wonderful way of approaching the craft and I think that as actors, we have to bring a full tool kit into all of our work. Also, I stress with my students when they come in, that everyone's uniqueness is what makes them a gift to their art. So if they want to be Tom Cruise, I let people know there's already a Tom Cruise, and there's already an Olivier, and there's already a Meryl Streep, a Dustin Hoffman, a Pacino and DeNiro. Somebody already took those parts and the student must find the ways of expressing their own uniqueness. So it's a combination of your uniqueness married with the tools that can be acquired through good training. I also think that you have to really want it. You can come in with a minimal amount of apparent talent and if you want it enough and you work hard enough, you're going to develop into a good actor. See, I believe that talent is a combination of instincts and craft. Sometimes, instincts are blocked by low self-esteem. My job is to chip away at the blockage so that the instincts of the actor can start coming through. At the same time, I enable the actor to have these wonderful tools that make the process easier. As soon as they start moving in this direction, their talent starts to show through. I've had people walk through the door who appeared to have all of the talent in the world and they never moved and never grew, because they just didn't want it enough. And I've had kids who walk through the door that people say, "But you're going to be stealing their money," and I'd say, "Just you wait and see." And they turn around to be the best people in the class. I work very much with the individual. I treat every actor who walks into my classroom according to their instrument. A mechanic who has a lot of cars brought in fixes each car according to what each individual car needs to make it run and to make it work at its best. And that's what I do in my classrooms.

I give my students the complete vocabulary, I don't give them my vocabulary. I will open them up to understand that Stella Adler says, "Action," where another teacher will say, "Go," and another teacher will say, "Need and want," and another teacher will say, "Objective," and they all mean exactly the same thing. I explain where each one of the words comes from and what their background is and what they represent to those people, so that when actors are reading material, they can translate what they're reading. I will do emotional recall work. I will do object work. I will do repetition. I will do exercises from the Royal Academy, which deal a lot with working from the outside in, as well as all of the work that we do from the inside out. I go heavily into script analysis. My class has become quite well-known for script analysis and the reason for that is because I have an enormous respect for the written word and what playwrights are trying to get across to the actor who is going to be bringing to life the characters and the situations that they've written. We work in-depth on the script; we do ten to fifteen pages a week where we just go in and explore. Sometimes we may spend a whole class just on one page of dialogue, getting into not only the intentions from the written word, but we get down into what is beneath everything that is being said.

The first thing that happens when we read a script is that we get a little motion picture in our head, and that's called our first impression. And our first impressions are, oh, maybe sixty to eighty percent of the time right, but that means that twenty to forty percent of the time, they're not right. I tell the actor, "Why take the chance?" You have to set that first impression off to the side and start re-reading the play. The first step is you pull out all of the facts, these are not suppositions; these are actual facts. Once you've pulled out all of the facts, the next thing you do is you marry facts. And after you've married the facts, you come up with a conclusion. It's when you come up with the conclusions that you start using your imagination. Then all of your creativity is based on a very strong foundation that is brought right back to the script itself. You know, the script is the seeds that your performance grows out of.

My scene study class is separated from my sensory/technique class. One I call the workout class, and it's like a dancer doing bar work. The scene study is like the dancer doing combination. You're only going to be as good in your combination as you are at the bar. I've heard too many actors say, "I've had classes. I've studied." I tell them right to their faces, "How absolutely arrogant. A singer never stops studying. A pianist never stops studying. Picasso was working his craft when he was 90 some odd years old, but you have had acting classes." (As you see, that's one of my buttons!) But actors have to remember that they have an instrument that needs to be kept limbered, that needs to keep being fine tuned and working at its top form, that they have to be stretching all of the time, that they have to go into areas that are uncomfortable.

One of my biggest strengths is teaching people how to get the job through the audition process. In my cold reading class, I spend the first three weeks with the actors myself going through the casting situation from A to Z. And for the last five weeks, I bring in a working, successful casting director. The casting director will get the pictures of the actors in class and he or she will choose the audition scenes for the students. And twenty-four hours before the audition, we give the students a call telling them that their sides are available to be picked up and we give them an audition time. When the actor comes in at his audition time, he has a one-on-one with the casting director, as he would if he went into that casting director's office. And we tape it. After each individual actor has had their individual auditions, everyone gets invited back in the room and we play back each one of the tapes. The casting director then critiques the actor in terms of whether or not they would have gotten a call-back, whether or not they would have been brought directly to the producer and the director. And if not, exactly why, with no holds barred, because if you're out there auditioning, then you have to be able to take the kind of critiquing that can go on in this particular environment. And once the casting director is finished, I will critique the actor in terms of the actor's growth and I will tell the actor what tools that actor needs to use in order to get to the result that the casting director was looking for.

When I interview prospective students, I am looking for need and want. The thing that I shy away from is arrogance. Some students come in and they think that they're going to get up onto a stage and I'm going to say, "Move left, move right, smile here, smile there, let's see a tear, thank you very much, here's your Academy Award." They don't understand that in my classes it's not about my creativity, it's not about my intelligence, it's not about anything that I can do—it's about what you do. And if you don't do the work, you suffer the consequences, I don't.

I really believe I was destined to teach. I love it and I love students. I love watching actors grow. I love watching them go through breakthroughs. I love watching them achieve things. I love seeing the transformation that happens in them as people. There's an enormous amount of trust that goes on in my school and I make myself very accessible to my actors. I don't hide behind an office door. Also, I never stop learning myself and I never teach the same class twice, because I would become bored. It would drive me crazy. If they say to me, "What if I never become an actor?" I turn around and say, "Listen, if you do this work and you work hard in this, even if you decide that you don't want this anymore, you're going to walk away a richer person."

The Students of Adam Hill

DICK VALENTINE

What has been most exciting in studying with Adam have been the whole new vistas opened up to me. Adam explains things to me that I have been doing automatically but never knowing why. I have had breakthroughs in class and I feel like a child with a new toy—eager and excited about my craft; as excited as I was when I started over forty odd years ago. I have more confidence now than I ever had. Adam has taken my weaknesses and made them strengths.

Adam is the consummate acting teacher. He has no ego, hard to believe I know, but he LOVES to teach. He is available, supportive, and understanding of an actor's problems and fears. I cannot praise this man too highly.

JENNIFER JANE RHODES

Working with Adam, I have become a great detective when I read the script. I have learned invaluable lessons in approaching character work, in making strong and interesting choices. I have stretched my instrument, released my inhibitions and truly learned how to prepare for a role.

Adam has a gentle approach that is so supportive. He has always been available to make sure I understand any of his instructions or critiques.

Adam Hill: The Facts

Adam Hill Workshop/Workout
4378 Lankershim Blvd.
Universal City, CA 91602
213-668-2034
213-208-3859

Length of time teaching: 25 years
Classes: Scene study, sensory/technique, script analysis, cold reading. Master and professional levels. Call for specific schedule.
Private Coaching: $60 per hour for individuals; $120 per hour (and up) if sent by studio
Admission: By interview (except for cold reading class, which requires an audition.)

Chapter 16
ANITA JESSE

The thing I'm most interested in is trying to produce actors who are independent of me and everyone else. I'm hoping not to dictate a pie-packaged system so much as I am in guiding an actor in his or her own quest for self discovery. I want actors to become independent and to discover their own method. I realize that sounds so vague. Does that mean then I just sort of turn them all loose and say listen to your inner voice? Nothing could be further from the truth. I'm doing a lot of training, but I'm hoping that each actor is finding his own way ultimately to a system that works for him or her.

One of the basic tenets in my teaching is that the creative process is something that springs out of that tension between limitation and freedom, so that's what I spend my energies on in the classroom. I'm trying to help the actor to understand the limitations of each individual role, how to read and analyze a script, how to determine what is the story, what is the playwright saying, what are the given circumstances, what are the character's needs, what are the discoveries, where are the transitions in the scene—all of that. But ultimately, I believe all preparation of any sort as an actor is designed to free the unconscious. So another whole set of exercises is aimed at that end of it—helping the actor to be freer, to learn to be playful, to learn to be spontaneous, to learn to trust themselves. I tell my actors, "I hope you can give up the idea of attacking a script and beating it into submission. At the same time, I don't want you to be the kind of an actor who is dependent solely on inspiration and intuition, because I think either of those two paths leads to disaster." I think it's a matter of combining the two. It's a matter of knowing how to do all that nitty gritty stuff that a lot of actors who are very much in touch with their intuition are afraid to get involved with because they're afraid it will stifle them. And my point is, "No, no, it will not stifle you. It's the opposite, it will set you free." But ultimately, if you become the kind of actor who only knows how to analyze, or becomes overly dependent on the analysis process, well I describe this as "paralysis by analysis." You can become so caught up in the analysis process and what you then are obligated to deliver, that you forget about allowing yourself to be spontaneous, to discover within the moment.

As a warm-up, I start out every class with some sort of game playing that's designed to help actors to make friends with that playful part of themselves and to know that they can be silly. I encourage them to make friends with making a fool of themselves in public so that they get over the fear of that. I use some common games like sound ball and machine and they start out usually being very cautious, with limited involvement of their bodies and their voices. But as they continue, the sounds get marvelously complex, they begin to use their bodies and they begin to fall in love with and develop an appetite for that moment when they have no idea what's going to happen next. I think it was Al Pacino who said to a young actress, "If you get an urge to act, just go lie down until it passes." Of course, it's the old business that everybody's trying to do, help them to get out of their heads and into their bodies.

The main event on the exercise platter is an exercise in which I give each actor one line of dialogue, and embedded in that line of dialogue is a specific need. So partly through the experience of it and partly through viewing other actors go through it, the students begin to understand how out of given circumstances, needs arise. This is not some formula that some acting teacher thought up, it's because that's how we work in real life. And then the needs will automatically produce actions. I call that finding your character's "psychic itch" because when that itch exists, you don't have to think about shall I or shall I not scratch. That psychic itch exists and it automatically compels the action.

I want my students to understand how to find the character's objective and how to commit to that need, that want, that desire. But I want them to understand that it is not the be all and the end all of acting. A lot of actors who are excellent at identifying an objective can articulate it with the best of them. And their work is cold and sterile because what they do is they fasten themselves to an objective and play it for all its worth throughout the entire scene, but there's never any interaction. And ultimately, of course, that is the goal, the interaction. If all I'm committed to is my objective and nothing you do affects me or changes me in anyway, why in heaven's name would anyone want to watch it? Committing to the objective is the jump start that starts the scene. Then you must be free to throw that out and totally change your objective at any given moment. Otherwise, it's not alive, it's not happening here and now. I'm always trying to get across to actors this concept that there's a trap for you as an actor that you'll be seduced into thinking that your job is to get up in front of the audience and act as sort of a guide, standing on the edge of the stage saying to the audience, "Now this is what would happen. It would go something like this, if this event..." And I'm saying, no, no, no, no. I don't want to watch that. I want to buy into the theatrical illusion that this is happening right here, right now. That it's never happened before, will never happen again. And you can't do that for me if you stand on the outside and understand every element of it.

I think my greatest strengths as a teacher are my commitment to starting with an actor where he or she is at this moment and also, my patience. I do not measure an actor against my image of where he or she should be, but I keep the actor moving forward. I like to think that my whole job is to keep moving that carrot further and further rather than to beat the actor up for not being where I want him to be. And I guess that one of my other strongest points is to go about the teaching with specifics. While Stanislavsky taught that generalities are the enemy of the actor, oh they are so much the enemy of the teacher. I like to give my actors specific tools to work with rather than this amorphous, "I want you to be free, I want you to be spontaneous." You know, a lot of acting teachers plug away at the idea that you must get your attention off of yourself. Well, you can tell students that until you're blue in the face, but until you substitute something for that, they're going to continue to do it because everybody's got to be somewhere. That actor's mind is going to be focused on some point of concentration and if it isn't on something specific that will help them as an actor, it will be on something destructive. So that's my focus—on action. "What's happening? Are you winning or are you losing? Are you getting what you want or are you failing to get what you want?"

When I interview, I spend a half an hour with a potential student actually working with them just as I would in a classroom situation. The actor does a cold reading and I give notes and the actor repeats the cold reading. I'm interested in whether or not my comments have made a difference. I'm interested in whether or not I can hear the actor and whether or not the actor can hear me. And I'm looking for that spark that tells me that our relationship is going to be a profitable one. I'm not so much looking for the skills of the actor is as I am for that spark.

I'm constantly amazed and I marvel at what wonderful human beings actors are. I love them. They're so creative, they're so generous, they're so warm and supportive, and one of my greatest blessings is having always attracted such wonderful actors. I treasure that atmosphere in the room of people supporting one another, celebrating one another's victories, experiencing the empathy in the room, hurting for other people when they're struggling, the respectful silences and the listening. It's a wonderful process to be part of. Sometimes I think, "Dare I ever let these people know that I probably should be paying them for this experience I'm having?" I'm also very much interested in actors succeeding in their craft and I would love every single one of them to get the lead in a series. Wouldn't that be wonderful? But I also want them to understand the bigger picture of struggling to be an artist in life. One of the actors I've worked with off and on through the years of whom I am most proud, is a gal who may never work professionally. She's not extraordinarily gifted as an actress, but what a fabulous human being and what passion she has for the craft. She works in community theater. She acts, she directs, she produces, and she's one of the people who's really doing the work. And so in her community, those individuals are seeing theater. And it's so popular, especially here in Los Angeles, for people to turn their noses up at those kinds of actors and I'll tell you, this gal directing a production of OF MICE AND MEN is of far more value in the long run to the human condition than a lot of the things being done on television. So I urge my actors to explore their gifts and to treasure those gifts and to use them in whatever way life takes them. If it's doing the lead in a series, so be it, God bless them. But if it isn't, God bless them as well.

The Students of Anita Jesse

CHRIS SLAGLE

Because of the respect and trust that Anita has generated in me, I am letting go of the fear of being human. That is, I am dealing fully with my emotions, physicality, and mentality as a whole. I am getting to know myself and most importantly learning to trust my instincts. I am removing my own performance anxiety-related arrogance and replacing it with true investment in situation and character. Anita's steady encouragement and patience, especially when I am frustrated with myself, has been very important to me. She reminds me that I do not have to be "excellent now" and that I am improving slowly and surely towards the goals I would like to achieve. Anita's ability to cut through the extraneous information and distill the vital points and present them for thought, discussion and practice, is invaluable.

During class, if a student is having difficulty, Anita is sensitive to the vulnerability the student feels and the chances they take. Anita has never berated anyone in class, rather she positively supports growth and gently steers the student in the right direction in moments of doubt or confusion. This environment, coupled with the inspiration I feel in Anita's classes, have convinced me that I am in the right place to grow as an actor and an individual.

JAYNE LEE HESS

Working with Anita, I have gained the courage and confidence to take risks. I now thrive on pushing beyond limits and exploring new territory. I have learned to set myself up for what I would least expect to happen to me as the character. I have learned to be vulnerable and I am no longer afraid to humiliate myself or to be laughed at as the character. I have also become open to where the scene takes me.

Anita is always available and supportive. I have always felt the freedom to stay late after class or call her at home any time I needed to talk with her or get advice from her regarding my career. I am so fortunate to study with Anita—she is brilliant.

CAROL WOODLIFF

Anita's classes are very practical. We mix cold reading, improvisation, scene study techniques and prepared scenes. Her classes are good training for the fast-paced world of television acting. I've learned to work quickly, make solid choices that propel me into the scene. I've learned to be ready for auditions and for anything that could be thrown at me on the set. I am also learning not to check myself to make sure I'm getting it right, but to trust that if I mix my life with the imagined reality of the character, I can be free to be real and let the work unfold without effort.

Anita's emphasis is on the positive, building on the good things you have and developing confidence by doing. Anita encourages us to support each other's growth and celebrate it as proof of each person's potential for great work. Anita builds people up, she is knowledgeable and generous and her goal is to help you become a better actor. Anita has encouraged my dream and she has helped me get closer and closer to being the type of actor I want to be.

Anita Jesse: The Facts

Anita Jesse Actors' Workshop
Gardner Stages
1501 N. Gardner Street
Los Angeles, CA 90046

Mailing Address:
859 Hollywood Way
Burbank, CA 91505
213-876-2870
818-767-4576

Length of time teaching: 20 years

Classes: Ongoing classes for professional, advanced, intermediate and beginning actors. Classes cover scene study, cold reading, on-camera technique, script analysis, monologues, audition technique, improvisation, exercise work and career counseling. Classes meet on Monday, Tuesday, Wednesday (two classes), and Thursday at 7:30PM and on Saturday at 11:00AM.

Private Coaching: $65 per hour (current students); $95 per hour (actors not enrolled in workshop)

Admission: By both audition and interview

Chapter 17
ERIC STEPHAN KLINE

As an undergraduate, I discovered videotape and got involved in the directing side of things. Then, I went and took a master's at San Francisco State in television production and produced and wrote and directed a bunch of pieces there, often times of necessity, starring myself. I guess I was suffering from the Orson Welles syndrome. When I came down to LA, I began working in production as a cameraman and an editor and sometimes a story consultant. And in a funny way, that is how I started at the workshop, because they needed somebody to work in the studio to videotape the scenes. But after about six months, I went to Tony Barr and said, "You really should have one person teaching both sides of the class." He said, "Well, we've never had anybody that could do that." But I was versed in acting and also in studio production. I said, "Well, next time you need a teacher, why don't you give me a shot?" So he gave me a shot and it seemed to work out, and then he gave me another class and that seemed to work out, and that was 16 years ago. So it's all been on-the-job training basically. It's now probably about 18,000 scenes later, the equivalent of 180 feature films or so.

Tony Barr has certainly been my mentor. Basically, everything I know, Tony taught me. Along the way, I've figured out more practical ways to implement his theories, but it's all based on his work. I always admired his practicality. Tony once said, "If I can't use something, I don't want to know about it. " His work is all very accessible and understandable to an actor. The thing that enhances this is that we work on video tape and we play the tapes back and we very carefully analyze what works and what doesn't work. Tony said that as an actor, especially in Hollywood on film and television, your uniqueness is what you have to sell—with all of your warts and with all of your moles. If you look at people like Hoffman or Bogart, they would be thrown out by any dramatic academy. They had bad speech patterns, they were too short and they just didn't fit the mold. But on camera, they light up because they're so definitively themselves.

My philosophy of teaching is pretty much Socratic. That's very old-fashioned, but I try to do as little direction as actually possible. I try to just formulate the questions of the role or of the scene and throw them back onto the actor for them to answer in their own terms. Most roles, especially film roles are structured in such a way that they'll accept a very wide latitude of responses and still honor the role and allow the piece to keep moving forward. I guess the prototype of this would be Hamlet. They're still figuring out new ways to do it after five hundred years, but still honor the basic text. And so what I am trying to do is get the actor connected to what's driving him in the role and then get as much of his own impulses into it as possible because that's where real life on the screen comes from. It doesn't come from some kind of cerebral plan of a performance, it comes from those moment-to-moment reactions. It's also important not to get tricked into theatricalizing the performance so it'll look right for an audience. Michael Caine says in his book that if you're rehearsing a scene well, you know it because the costume guy will come up in the middle of it and say, "Which jacket, this one or that one?" because he thinks you're just talking. Caine says that you know you're in trouble when you're rehearsing a scene and you look around and the whole crew is standing in rapt attention because what you've done is you've inadvertently made them into an audience and then theatricalized the scene. And it won't look very good on camera.

So, I think one of my strengths as a teacher is my sensitivity to working with performances and then translating them to the camera. My other strength is a knowledge of story and script and so it's fairly easy for me to get people to understand what their role is and how certain choices are possible or not possible given the overall architecture of the script. I also do a lot of private coaching. The work here is not too much different than the work that we do in class, it just has to be done faster because these people usually get their script somewhere between twelve and twenty-four hours before they're going to audition. And again, it's all about getting people connected. I help them to "bottom line the scene," in other words, to make a really simple statement of what their goal or need is in the scene and then to connect to it. This will give them an edge up in terms of getting the job. A major casting director came into the workshop and did a Q&A and I asked, "Well, what do you look for in a reading?" And she said, "Well, it's always nice when an actor makes a choice." I said, "Well what do you mean, like a rich choice or a really active choice?" She said, "Oh, no, no. Just a choice. You know, ninety percent of the actors that come into read for me, they just read. They haven't done any of that." And so, if you do one or two or three of those elements and by chance connect with them, you've already leap-frogged your way into the top ten percent of the people reading for the part.

In class, I do an exercise which I call "talk-back." It's based on the idea that there are really no monologues on camera. Everything is a dialogue. It's just that, especially in film, only about a quarter of your actual responses are being underlined by written words. As an illustration, I'm talking to you right now and you're probably thinking, "Oh, that's interesting. What does he mean by that? Oh, boy, I've heard that a million times before. Oh, that's ridiculous. Oh wait, wait a minute, that could be fun." There's a constant editorial commentary going on, a stream of responses. And to get actors to do that, I have them convert all the monologue passages in a film to dialogue by having them speak out or talk back their responses, so that the listener gets connected to what he's thinking and feeling moment-by-moment and the speaker gets connected to the resistance that he's trying to overcome in that moment. And then when you go silent you have a life on screen in between the lines. And I have various other ways of raising the moment-to-moment responses to the surface.

We work in a video studio and we cold read, we rehearse and then we videotape scenes. So the workshop is run like what would happen on a set rather than in a classroom, because I figure I'm not preparing these people for a classroom—I'm preparing them for the set. People aren't allowed to talk while we're in serious rehearsal or when we're taping, but other than that, there's a lot of milling around and it's quite informal. I encourage people to ask questions and make random comments and do all the things that happen in what you would call "the real world," because I find that the normal structure of classrooms is very stultifying. And the last thing you want to do to an actor is put him in a position where he has to sit on his impulses. I am always trying to create a community within which people can do good work. When that is working, it creates a kind of group dynamic that makes everybody's work better. I'm not a very good disciplinarian. I believe that the students have to want to be there or they shouldn't be there and there's just no way of making them want to be there if they don't.

The Students of Eric Stephan Kline

HEATH KIZZIER

Eric makes the whole concept of acting understandable and attainable. Instead of giving you the easy answer, he will guide you in such a way that you are the one who figures out what you are doing in a scene. I have learned from Eric how to listen, how to be truthful, how to make choices and how to follow them through. Working with Eric has been invaluable; he has made me a much better actor.

ERIC BRUSKOTTER

Working with Eric, I have learned to be simple, honest and specific. I have also learned that listening is everything and the importance of when to throw away the preparation and return to playing the scene moment-to-moment. Eric constantly challenges me and is always there for me. I find that I am now much more confident, free and relaxed in my work. I also appreciate that Eric is extremely positive and enthusiastic.

KRISTINA GRONSETH

One of the most exciting moments that I have experienced in Eric's class was the first time that I cried on camera. The excitement didn't come from the fact that tears came out of my eyes, but that it was the first time I felt comfortable and free enough on camera to lose myself in the role.

Eric goes out of his way to be available to us. He is extremely patient and he always makes me feel that we are on the same level. Working with Eric, I have become confident enough to risk being open and vulnerable in my work. Eric is a wonderful teacher and respected by everyone in our class.

Eric Stephan Kline: The Facts

Film Actor's Workshop
2050 South Bundy Drive, Suite 100
Los Angeles, CA 90025
310-442-9488
310-575-4055

Length of time teaching: 15 years.
Classes:
    Beginning
    Tuesday   7:30PM – 10:30PM
    Thursday   7:30PM – 10:30PM
    Advanced
    Monday   7:30PM – 10:30PM
    Wednesday 7:30PM – 10:30PM
Private Coaching: $50 per hour.
Admission: By interview

Chapter 18
ALLAN MILLER

The first training period of my life, was at the Dramatic Workshop when it was run by a man named Erwin Piscator who was Bertold Brecht's mentor. As a total neophyte, having no knowledge or experience except for having been in a couple of plays in the Army and one in college, I was dazzled, amazed, provoked and stimulated in ways I couldn't even imagine before I was under the influence of this man. And it wasn't so much the classroom technique thing, because he did very little of that. It was the productions that he did. To see what he wrought with a written piece of material has kept me feeling enthusiastic and decisive about wanting to stay in theater as long as I have. It was a mixture of humanity and social concerns that he brought, even to Shakespeare productions, that were unflaggingly brilliant and incisive and deeply moving.

I then went to study with Uta Hagen, whom I idolized. I was in a class with Geraldine Page, Joan Hackett and Bill Hickey and the main influence I got from Uta was the ability to kind of direct myself in the scene by being able to break it down into component parts that were actable. However, there was something that kept happening in that class that put something in my still young fancies about the mystery and wonderment of an artist at work. It's different than intelligent, reasonable ways of going about dealing with things in acting terms. And Geraldine Page was the key to it. It was something that she did in everyone of her pieces that was a little bit more and other than what the rest of us seemed to be doing. We all got very confident and adroit and our scenes began to take on real life, with a sense of action and conflict. But whenever Geraldine worked, there was something else going on that none of us, including Uta, could put our finger on. It has taken me many, many years to really discover and focus on what that was.

After Uta's, I went to the Actor's Studio. I didn't really want to go there but it was free and my money had run out and Uta couldn't afford to give me a scholarship any longer. My wife had an audition for the Studio and her partner fell out at the last minute and she begged me to do it and so I did. It was an awful experience, but we both passed and got in. Then I began to observe at the studio with my wife because we were petrified to get up and work in front of anybody, as most new people were. The people were rather cruel, you had to get up and prove your desire and where-withal—otherwise, they weren't very warm and welcoming. I soon became a kind of a big-mouth at the studio. I would put my hand up to make comments about almost everybody's work and Strasberg began to notice me and point at me and say, "Well, what do you have to say, Allan? What would you like to say?" And partly it was a joke and partly he was en-couraging me. Finally, I did get up and do a scene and Strasberg turned to me and said, "You have a very interesting manner. I don't know if I believe it or not, but do another scene." I walked out feeling like King Shit think-ing, "I fooled Strasberg. I fooled Strasberg, I fooled…what do I mean I fooled Strasberg…wait a minute, what am I doing here?" And I began to wonder, "What does he mean that I have good stage manner, what does he mean that he doesn't know if he believes it or not?" So I had to become more truthful. I thought I was being truthful, but he demanded some-thing more of me, and his demands I wanted to meet.

So I began experimenting and years later, I did an experiment at the studio where instead of trying to do the objectives and the regular kind of tasks and sensory/emotional things, I made a list of all the things that I could find in the script that I was working on about this character. If the character said he was a writer, then I said, "OK, I have to practice being a writer." He said he had a will that his wife had left him, so one night I stayed up late and wrote an imaginary will that I thought my wife might have left to me if something happened to her and so on. I had a list of these things and I asked my scene partner to please go along with me, and she said, "Sure." I didn't know what I was going to do with these things, but I knew that during the course of the scene as I said my dialogue, I was going to have to do something to relate to each of these things on my list. At the end of it, Strasberg swung around at me with this wonderful smil-ing, beaming look on his face and said, "Before anybody says anything, I want to know how many people here think Allan was doing one task with a lot of variations or if he was doing a lot of different tasks?" Before any-body could say too much, he said, "I thought it was one task with a lot of different…" and I went, "No, no, no. It was all different ones." And he was very curiously taken aback and he said, "What do you mean?" And I said, "Oh, I had a list of things that I was doing." And he said, "Oh was that that piece of paper you kept looking at?" And I said, "Yes." And he said, "Well, so what's on the list?" And I started reading a couple of the things to him and all of a sudden he said, "Well, you were standing over there and all of a sudden you started to shiver, what was that?" I said, "Oh no, that was not on the list. I was going from one numbered thing on my list to the next one." And he suddenly stopped and he said, "Uh-huh, from now on try to do more of what happens to you in between the numbers." And then I knew what it was that Geraldine Page had been doing. It was what happened to her while she was working on the part that she allowed into the role. And that was a huge insight for me, it was the major turning point in both my acting and teaching life. And I've been on that singular aspect of the creative process ever since.

Everyone of us is an individual. There's no way in the world that two different people being asked to do the same thing should come out the same way. And yet, I see actor after actor struggle to try to make it come out the way the director says he wants it or the way the actor thinks it should be. And then the creative process is gone, lost by an individual who once was fresh and original. And the metaphor for that for me is always children's drawings. Billions and billions of children's drawings have been done since recorded time and no matter what culture, the subjects in their drawings are always the same within their culture. The subjects are always the same, yet every single drawing is original. That's what keeps me focused and functioning and that's what I'm looking to keep available to whoever I work with.

The kind of techniques that I have learned to use, I've changed drastically since I've had to be in Los Angeles, because so many of the people that come to study here are so used to their idea of being in TV and film. I have to tell them that when they get to TV and film here, they will have no rehearsals. They'll go over lines and blocking, but that's not a rehearsal of anything. So if they don't have their own criteria for being creative and imaginative in what they do after waiting sometimes eight to ten hours in a little cubicle, waiting to be called to perform; if they don't know how to adapt themselves immediately to a situation in which the way they read for the part is almost never the way the director then suggests that they do it on the set—then they become a cipher. So some of the techniques that I use now are to help deal with this situation in particular. How you go about rehearsing a part, when you get it one night and have to come in the next morning and start doing it, is truncated. It's different. Even though the the parts of yourself that you use may be the same, you have to use yourself differently. And you have to be prepared to adapt to whatever is there at the time when you do it, and still stay creative.

For instance, for the long waits when you're in your cubicle, I always suggest you go in and visit the set that you're going to be working on and try to think of you, yourself, as the character in those circumstances and what kind of life you might lead in that environment. Also, I suggest that you look around wherever you are, including your cubicle, or take a little walk around outside the cubicle and ask yourself, "Is there anything in this room, in this space, or outside this space that reminds me of the setting of the situation that the character is in?" So you start comparing where you are to the place that the action takes place in and even when you're listening or talking to other people, to see what subjects they are talking about that might have anything to do with what your character's subjects are. Let's say that in the scene you are going to do you are a doctor who has to make a decision that could affect the life or death of your patient, and it's a procedure that's new to you but you're going to try it because there's no other way to deal with it. And you're walking around outside and people are talking about the weather. How can you suggest to yourself that them talking about the weather might have anything to do with your life threatening situation? Yes, it could if the people are talking about how calm it is out, how bright and warm and easy. Then you think about the earthquake that just hit here a year and a half ago and could come at anytime now. If an earthquake were to come, how might you deal with it? And you put yourself into a frame of mind of relating to a life threatening situation. Not the literal one that's in your material, but the one that can absorb you, the one that can keep you tuned to that material that you're going to be acting. You're comparing, you're relating, you're asking yourself what is like what I'm going to be doing, what is unlike what I'm going to be doing, and you can do that for hours and not run out of material. This seems to me to be a very natural process that goes on all the time in our lives. So I'm applying it to the acting situation. I'm saying, "How could this foreign situation, this certain set of circumstances, this trailer with all the trucks and the cars and people suggest anything to me about the 'country' of my script, where I'm coming from, what I've studied, what I've looked over, what I've thought about, what I've tried to live with? What's like that, what's unlike that?" And you keep this process alive instead of getting stale by going over and over the material you're going to act. Most of all, this will keep your imagination alive and that's the key to me.

The principle of acting that I'm trying to apply in a lot of these things is, "Here am I, the artist, the actor wanting to act this scene that's foreign to me. It's written by someone else. It comes from someone else's imagination. Here am I. There is it." So how do you get two separate forces together in life? And one of the images that came to my mind was from chemistry. It's called a catalyst. A catalyst is something you use that helps put two disparate elements together, or helps pull them apart. So I said, "OK, for me to arrive at that piece of material instead of directly trying to get into it, why don't I look for something that allows me to, or awakens me to it?" Sometimes it's something you see, or something you hear. When a student asked Hemingway, "How do you make up your stories?" He said, "I make up my stories out of everything and anything I have seen, heard, read, or imagined. How would you?" And that still seems to me to be crucially true. So in my classes, I'm looking for people to get in touch with their own natural personal expressiveness. I'm not so much concerned with the things that you may have heard from Strasberg in the past, like private moments or personal experiences. What I am concerned with is using a personal place, image, experience, sound, piece of music, painting, from which to say, "Now that I'm thinking of that thing that's personal, what do I think of this piece of material?" It's always the movement to the material, not to get them to be more personal about themselves.

With new students, I usually do a little phone interview. If I need to, I go further and have a personal interview, or I'll invite somebody to read a portion of my book *A Passion For Acting*. I say, "Go to Samuel French and stand in the store and just read the first six or eight pages, and if you find that provocative and interesting, give me a call. When I do an interview, I'm trying to see if there's an awakened capacity in this person, if they're not so protective about themselves that they are unwilling to allow something to ruffle the patterns that they're in. One of the things I say over and over to everybody is, "The only thing that's in the way of your expressing yourself as an artist are your personal and social habits that are against individual expression." You see, I am a working actor who still makes his living as an actor and has been doing it for 35 or more years. If not for that, I wouldn't know about all these pressures that I've now made part of my vocabulary of teaching. And after all these years, I know that if any individual has enough appetite and discipline, I can teach them to act pretty good. If they don't have that appetite, there's no point.

The Students of Allan Miller

SUTHERN HICKS

The most important and useful idea I have learned in Allan's class is that there is no character on stage. I am on stage. It is my body, my thoughts and my past experiences. Unless I bring what is happening to "me" into what I am saying and doing as the character, the end result won't be very interesting or real. This has given me the ability to enjoy acting in a way that I never knew possible and has been of most value to me...so far.

DANA HUBBARD

Before working with Allan, I was so preoccupied with my characters inner emotional life and sense memories that I was detached from my fellow actor in the scene. Allan would say, "make it about them, make it about them." So Allan was most helpful in getting me to address this rather narcissistic attitude that had clouded my work. Allan also helped me to break down my own behavioral habits so that I can fully serve the requirements of the material and of the character. This has made acting so fresh and exciting for me.

JAN MARIE

The most important thing I have learned from Allan is that I must constantly work my instrument, keep it loose; to discover new ways of exploring and moving my body and my voice everyday. Allan is exciting and passionate and every week I watch my classmates grow. I am convinced that he is the best teacher in L.A.

Allan Miller: The Facts

Private classes held in Studio City
818-907-6262

Length of time teaching: 35 years
Classes:
     Monday   7:30PM – 10:30PM
Private Coaching: $125 per hour
Admission: By interview or recommendation

Chapter 19
LARRY MOSS

The very first training that I acquired was at a place called A.M.D.A. It was a school designed to ready people to enter musical theater specifically, and that was something that I loved and wanted to learn how to do. My acting teacher there was Sanford Meisner. I'm so grateful that Sandy's was my first acting technique because he trained me in finding my performance through being sensitive to the other actor's behavior. And so I learned early on, I was 19 years old, to leave myself alone. I really believe that Sandy's work is the best possible work to start with because it makes you truthful right away, and then you can build on that. I went on to study with Bill Tuttle and Charles Nelson Reilly and then I began working with Warren Robertson. Warren had worked extensively with Lee Strasberg and he felt that Lee didn't answer a lot of pertinent questions that had to do with how to get at emotionality through the body. And so he developed a series of exercises where very basic, physical choices create emotionality just by the physical action. That was very helpful for me because I was so physically inhibited. When I was able to really use my body non-verbally, I got in touch with something very powerful and it helped change me into a more creative actor.

Warren was the teacher that asked me after two years of studying with him whether I'd be interested in teaching. Interestingly enough, once I began to teach, it created a lot of confidence in me. In fact, the minute I started teaching, I began to work on Broadway with people like Neil Simon, Michael Bennett, Jerome Robbins, Gene Saks and Gerald Friedman. So the combination of studying and actually working in the theater with great artists started to make me feel that I had some kind of basis to feel confident in. I also started therapy when I was 20 and stayed in it for many years, and for me the therapeutic process has helped me to consolidate my own self. I had a background that was somewhat difficult and my mother was mentally ill which had a certain impact upon me, both good and bad. Good in that it made me highly sensitive to other people's behavior, because when you're living with someone whose behavior changes on a dime, you learn to listen and watch very carefully.

Once I began to teach and work more, I realized that there was something lacking, and that was helped finally by working with Stella Adler. In terms of having a mentor, someone that I think back on who is constantly with me, it is Stella. She taught an extraordinary class called "Script Interpretation" and I was with her for three years. As we studied the great playwrights, Stella would take us into their social times. She helped us understand who the playwright was as a human being, why they wrote what they wrote and what the social and political ideas behind the play are. Once you understood why Arthur Miller was writing DEATH OF A SALESMAN, what happened after the industrial revolution and how certain jobs became superfluous, you start to see that Willy Loman had no reason for being. That what was once a job in which people would visit different small towns and sell things, once automation came in, they weren't necessary anymore. You really started to see Willy's point of view in America. We worked on PYGMALION by George Bernard Shaw and Stella made us understand that when Eliza Doolittle says, "Yeoow," and all those funny sounds when she takes the bath, that in England at that time, a woman of that social economic class never took a bath with hot water. She didn't know what warm water was. So those sounds aren't about being funny, they come from stark terror and poverty because she thinks she's either going to be frozen to death or scalded to death. You know, once I began to be educated about the playwrights, I would sit in her class and weep, because she answered questions about where to find character and where character really comes from in people's backgrounds.

My philosophy in training actors is that you start with the human being that's standing in front of you and all of the things that have made that person who they are: their vitality; their generosity of spirit; their imagination; their humor; and their life force. I like to tap into that excitement that they had when they first said, "I want to be an actor," because it comes from a burst in the person that says, "I must use my body. I must use my voice. I must use language. I must speak from myself about life." It may start out as a visceral need to be seen or to exorcise demons within them, but finally, once those emotions are connected to writing, that's when the actor takes off.

I demand my students read the great plays. We only work in class on the good writing, because I know that when my students go out and work, they will know enough about script analysis to extrapolate from what might be a mediocre script and find the important nuggets. I'll give you an example. There was an actor I was working with on a new play and it was a very long, talky scene and he was very dull in it. And I said, "Well, what are the clues about the character?" And there was one word and the word was "cheerleader." He had been a cheerleader because he couldn't play football, and that was a clue to the vitality and the desire of the character. And once that clue was found, it informed the whole performance.

An acting choice must create a physical impulse. And if it doesn't create something that you want to do physically, it's not really usable. You may or may not choose in the moment to act on it because of the circumstances of the scene, but you must want to. That's what creates a living body on the stage and when I think of great performances, I don't think so much of what they said, I think of something about their physicality—I remember the way they stood, or a look on their face. Acting is a physical experience and I do a lot of statue work. For instance, a student will start with a relaxation exercise and then I'll say, "If what you're feeling inside could be externalized in the statue, what would that physical life be?" And then the student would go to that physical life. And then I say, "What does that physical life produce in you emotionally and where does it make you want to go next?" And we'll go to another statue. And we usually do that four or five times. And what you begin to find, as in all character, is that every human being wants to go up—like in nature, everything goes towards the sun. Well, human beings do, too. We want to love, we want to reach out, we want to get what we want but life sometimes smashes you so that you can't. Something gets in the way which creates neurosis, and that's character. I think once the student understands that in their own life, they begin to have an empathy for all characters.

One of the things I'm aware of with a lot of actors, particularly when they begin, is that they stop the breath. When people break through in acting, the breath gets free. And so one of the things I start with is making the student aware of where their breath is coming from in their bodies. From that, we work on the awareness of where they hold tension in their body on a day-to-day basis. Once they breathe into that tightness and release it, emotion will come up because we hide emotions in muscles. it's phenomenal to me to watch how much emotion is immediately available. You know, people worry in acting about being emotional, but your attention must be on what you're doing and doing it fully. And you need an instrument that is free to breathe.

I try to do as many different things as I can because you don't know what is going to tap into each actor. I find certain actors are incredibly responsive to sensory work. Other actors are incredibly responsive to mirror work. Some people need to use just their imagination. If an actor says to me, "I used something personal from my life," and it works for them and it doesn't take them out of the play or upset them in a destructive way, that's not bad technique. It's as good as when someone uses something completely imaginary or uses something imaginary about someone real in their life. In other words, I don't judge what people use. I don't think a teacher should be dogmatic about what students use to create emotional life. I think that's intrusive, uncreative and egotistical on the teacher's part. You have to respect the actor and find out what's great for them and then support that. Then you give them a new idea and, who knows, it might lead them to an enormous break-through. After all of the exercise work, then I get into script analysis and all of the fundamental who, what, why, when and where questions that the actor must answer. And to me, the best actors are the people who ask the best questions. So those are things I break down very, very clearly and specifically. And then of course, once you've done all that work, it's worthless unless you show up and listen and hear the other person.

I don't interview or audition prospective students. I look at the picture and resume, I look at what they've done and who they've trained with and I get a sense of the student and I invite them into the class. You can tell within a month whether I'm the right teacher for them and if they're the right student for me. My students have to work very hard. The impression is that actors who are pursuing a film and television career in Hollywood are not still serious regarding their growth as actors. Not true, I have a core of people who are on fire. And I have a burning desire to contribute. Theater and film gave me a life, gave me a road, and it gave me everything that's good in my life. It gave me focus, discipline and emotional truth. It fed me, and I want to return that, because I feel that once people find if they have the taste for it, they can build an incredible life as actors. And when I help people bring good writing to life, I feel my reason for being on the planet has some value. Also, I enjoy the simple human listening to each other—because the relationship between the teacher and the student is one of incredible trust. And once a student trusts you, something extraordinary happens. They change, they grow, and I love that.

The Students of Larry Moss

MICHELLE DANNER

Larry's focus encompasses thorough script analysis, sensory realities, use and endowment of place and objects and the magic of clear intentions. The exciting part of the work is that it centers on the characters physicality and finding psychological gestures that illuminate the inner life of a role. One of Larry's greatest assets is that he works individually with the actors physical and emotional blocks. He sees each actor as a unique talent and he fosters the idea that by hard work and the power of observation, both personally and environmentally, the actor can thrive in his craft.

Larry's vast knowledge of theatre and film, his passion for the work, in addition to his own desire to continue to grow make him a source of inspiration for all of us. As an actress, he has taught me how to trust my instincts—which is the most valuable tool one can ever have.

REED DIAMOND

Larry's gift is his sensitivity and at the same time, how tenacious he is in getting actors to go beyond their fear, beyond their comfort level. He intuitively knows the next step each actor needs to take and he knows the correct and very personal way to push them in that direction. I now know how to create a role, bring a scene to life, and I have a toolbox to solve my acting problems when they arise.

Larry's passion for teaching and helping actors is incredible. His enthusiasm only increases as class goes on and he is always intently focused on each actor's work. Larry has given me a technique that helps me go deeper when I think my work is done and he has returned to me my joy of acting.

JASON GEDRICK

I had some early success as an actor, even a lot of attention and fan mail after the movie *Iron Eagle* was released. But something didn't feel right; I was faking it and I needed technique. The most profound realization I've ever had as an actor happened when I was working with Larry on an audition. In the past, I had been playing general qualities in the characters I portrayed by racing through the dialogue and emphasizing the obvious dramatic words without coming up for air. But as we worked, Larry looked at me and said, "breathe." What breathe meant for me was, take the time to experience what the character needs to experience and don't pretend to feel the lines. Larry has taught me that when I'm clear and very specific, I will be alive physically even when I am still. I have also learned how much fun it is to play with the element of the dangerous unknown.

Larry encourages us to be bold. The environment he creates allows us to be brave; brave enough to fail and brave enough to overcome our fears and anxieties because we know that we are safe from judgement. Larry's class is specific, positive and productive; it is a collaboration, where everyone feels they have the right to contribute.

Larry Moss: The Facts

The Larry Moss Studio
1242 3rd Street Promenade
Santa Monica, CA 90405
310-393-3801

Length of time teaching: 23 years
Classes: (Not all classes are taught by Larry. Call for details.)

Advanced

Monday	6:30PM	–	10:30PM
Wednesday	6:30PM	–	10:30PM
	1:00PM	–	6:00PM

Intermediate

| Tuesday | 6:30PM | – | 10:30PM |
| Thursday | 6:30PM | – | 10:30PM |

Beginning

| Saturday | 11:00AM | – | 4:00PM |

Private Coaching: Variable fees, call for details.
Admission: By picture, resume, and interview.

Chapter 20
TRACY ROBERTS

I got a lead on Broadway with no training, which is certainly not an example that I would set for anyone, but I had come down to New York from school on a vacation and I got the ingenue lead in a play with the Group Theater. I didn't know what the Group Theater was or who they were. I lived in a small town in upstate New York, and I had been in a high school play, but I ignored the drama department at school. And on this vacation, I got this part in PARADISE LOST by Clifford Odets and directed by Harold Clurman. Sandy Meisner was in the play, Stella Adler played my mother-in-law, and Morris Carnovsky played my father-in-law. So here were all these brilliant, incredibly well-trained people, and here I was. And I survived it. I opened on Broadway and I got some marvelous notices. When I went home, my mother told me that I had to have legitimate training if I wanted to be an actress, so I went back to New York and I started to study with Lee Strasberg. And I was so young, so untrained, and I didn't have great concentration, and I found the training to be extremely destructive for me personally. It was like very bad therapy with no solution. And it resulted in making me quite ill emotionally and physically and in every other way. I then got a contract in Hollywood, but I didn't know what I was doing, and I was fortunate enough to be sent to Michael Chekhov. Michael Chekhov was an absolutely brilliant angel. He completely emancipated me as an actress, and he restored my confidence. He taught me so much, and I feel so blessed that I was exposed to his teaching.

I never wanted to teach and I had no intention of teaching—I was living a very spoiled actress life. And then I went through a personal transition, and I started teaching a very small group of people who asked me to work with them, and it just simply grew like topsy! It was an incredible thing. I never advertised and people were lined up for classes—it was wonderful, it was exciting. And I don't know how to explain it except that I felt inspired and I had tremendous enthusiasm, so I think I inspired the students. The small studio I rented became too small and I began renting larger and larger places. Then, through my family, who were producers and writers, I started directing television, and that of course, brought more people in. So everything seemed to work together very fortuitously.

At the bottom of my staircase I have two inscriptions written. One of them is by Chekhov, which says, "To create by inspiration, one must be aware of one's own individuality." And the other one is by Goethe, who says, "After all our studies, we acquire only that which we put into practice." And I think that those two quotes are totally the basis of what I've tried to do in my teaching. I try to give people a personal way of working, an organized system of behavior that works for them under any and all circumstances. And you know how difficult it is to work under pressure on the set, for instance, when you're nervous and directors are just giving you external directions. Actors need to do the work for themselves first and then for other people. I strongly believe in sensory work, and I have found a way to teach it so that the actor doesn't become lost in the emotion, but he is able to feel it, control it, use it, shape it, and finally have it as something in his toolbox. I also believe in improv work and the actors learn to use improv based on what scenes they're doing. A lot of people will get tremendous results from working with Chekhov's "psychological gesture." This is a way of creating a strong, physical movement, which to the actor denotes a certain attitude. Let's say you are working on sense of power, you would go to a gesture that illustrates that—Chekhov would use a simple thing like chopping down a tree, just to give you the form of the movement. Once your body gets into the form of the movement, the actor works with it until he or she begins to find a gesture that for him or her expresses a general sense of power. They will then repeat that movement and ultimately, the movement is dropped and they can begin to communicate on a simple level. You find that this movement energizes you, it gives you expansion on stage.

I expose the actor to many ways of building a set of tools with which they will know themselves, know what responses they have to certain stimuli—whether it's external or internal. It's the way you respond that gives you your behavior. And if you organize that behavior into a system, then you begin to have a technique. And the point is that, you know, Jesus said it, Socrates said it, you have to know your own instrument before you can go to the so-called characters And hopefully, you make a marriage with that character so that it comes through you.

I teach the professional classes at my studio and I try to do two things with the actors. I try to make them stretch as much as they can stretch and do things that they would not be cast in. And then I try to make them work on contemporary things that they're doing every day in television and film. I guess my strength as a teacher, and what people tell me, is that I have a marvelous eye. I know immediately what's wrong and I know how to fix it. And I know how to coach in such a way that the student is able to use the information to enhance their technique. Also, I don't allow my students to be lazy. You know, so many actors make very little demands on themselves or on their partners. When they get a film or a television show, they just hope against hope that their partner is going to be satisfying or inspiring, and they don't know how to intensify their own reality, they don't do their homework. And it's very disappointing to me. I find a lot of truthful actors who are boring as hell; it could be done in somebody's living room and who cares?

To get into my class an actor must interview first and then they do two monologues, a contemporary and a classic. I look for someone that can make me sit up on the edge of my chair. I look for someone who involves me through their knowledge, through their technique, through their ability to put their persona into the work. I look for freedom, that they are putting to use their mind, body, spirit and that they are not working just from their head. And in the class, I believe strongly in discipline without having it be inhibiting. The atmosphere is very supportive; I don't allow any negativity. And the class is enthusiastic, my students come to work and they want to work. If someone comes to study with me, I want them to learn an independent craft and I want them to grow and never stop growing. I want them to go out into the world with a strong sense of security so that even if they don't get the part in that moment, that they know damn well they've done the best they can do.

The Students of Tracy Roberts

VALERIE DE ROPP

Tracy has helped me to improve and build on the skills I already had. She has enabled me to go more deeply into the mind, body and soul of the character as she requires that I really believe and justify everything that I say and do.

Before studying with Tracy, I never had a teacher (acting or otherwise) that actually called me at home to see how I was doing, to ask what scenes I was working on and to offer suggestions, support and encouragement. She has marvelous insight and wisdom and she has confidence in her students. Tracy's no-nonsense way of working gets you off your butt to do the work and to challenge yourself.

DEBRA RICH

The most important point Tracy stresses is to bring your own unique and honest self to any role you approach. She highly values creativity and instinct and encourages all of her students to find the deepest personal truth in any situation. Tracy also recognizes that many of us have specific talents which have brought us to a certain level of success in the business. While she nurtures those talents, she pushes us not to rely too heavily on them. Stretching is important to her. Tracy wants all of us to be great actors, not just soap stars.

Tracy is totally open to any and all creative ideas we may have about the work or the business. She encourages us to do readings and to use the theatre space when we can. She also brings in top casting and producing professionals to lead seminars and to meet her students. Tracy has given me a place to try new things fearlessly and she is one-hundred per cent supportive of my dreams and goals.

CLAUDINE GAUTIER

Tracy has taught me that when I ask the right questions, I feed my inner life. I have also learned specificity from her and that when I know what I am doing, the emotion takes care of itself. Tracy always focuses on the process rather than the end result which has given me great freedom to "work out" my acting instrument without any pressure to perform.

Tracy is extremely supportive of my needs not only as an actor, but as a human being struggling with life, pain, happiness, tragedy, etc. She calls to check in on me and I know that she is genuinely concerned. As a teacher and as a person, Tracy is exceptional.

Tracy Roberts: The Facts

Tracy Roberts Actors Studio
141 South Robertson Boulevard
Los Angeles, CA 90048
310-271-2730

Length of time teaching: 25 years
Classes: Basics, Scene Study I, Scene Study II, Professional Class, Audition Technique, Soap Workshop, Casting Directors Workshop, Speech, Movement. Please call studio to find out which classes Tracy is teaching and her specific schedule.
Private Coaching: $150 per hour
Admission: By interview and audition

Chapter 21
JEAN-LOUIS RODRIGUE

I trained as an actor in New York City with Herbert Berghof at the HB Studio and with Sonia Moore, who taught the Stanislavsky system. Sonia brought an Alexander teacher into her class to teach us and that was the first time I came across the Alexander techniques. I was 19 years old and I had a lot of bad habits. I had allergies, asthma and breathing problems that affected my voice as an actor very seriously. And the Alexander work had fantastic results—my voice improved, my stooped shoulders improved and I felt much better in my body. I was so impressed, that I started taking private Alexander lessons as well. Several years later, I got a scholarship at the American Conservatory Theater in San Francisco and when I went to study there with the company, I found out that the whole company was based on the Alexander technique. William Ball, the artistic director, was so clear about the power of the Alexander technique to stimulate a certain kind of physical life in the actor that he had everybody take Alexander technique lessons: the actors, the technicians, the administration of the theater, and of course, all of us in the training program. Frank Ottiwell was my Alexander teacher there and he was so impressive to me in terms of a teacher, an actor, and a mentor, that I seriously thought about becoming an Alexander teacher while I was working at ACT. But I spent some years working as an actor before I decided that the Alexander technique was the thing that really impressed me the most. So I went back to ACT in 1977 where I was accepted into a three-year Alexander teaching program being offered by Frank Ottiwell and I became an Alexander teacher. A few years later, I was also inspired by Margerie Barstow who was the first teacher trained by Mr. Alexander in 1931. Margerie was a very big influence in my application of the Alexander technique and how I teach it.

The Alexander technique has taught me that there are several basic processes that have to happen, and those processes are procedures that I actually practice myself. The one thing that I begin with is to really be clear about what you're seeing, what you're feeling and to be more aware of yourself and what is happening in the moment. When you can open your eyes and observe clearly and sense what's happening, then you begin to understand what has to happen next. The fundamental life of the actor is the presence of the actor in his body: seeing, listening, feeling, sensing, smelling, and being in the space that you're in. That's one of the basic principles of the Alexander technique—awareness. The second thing that I work a lot at is being able to make choices, having clarity in what direction you want to go in. When you know what's happening, and you know who you are and what you want, then you begin to be able to move into the directions that you want to go into. A lot of people have habits, including myself, and it takes a whole lifetime to be able to recognize the force of habit. Those habits may not be the habits of a character that you're portraying. So you have to make a distinction between your own habits and the habits of a character, because what shapes a character are a series of habits that are based on the conditions that the character's living in. The third thing is to learn how to direct one's energy. It's difficult to cultivate, yet everyone has that ability to direct their physical, mental and emotional energy. You need to do that to be able to act—how can you fulfill an objective if you can't really fulfill that direction within your own body?

The Alexander technique is very intimate work, literally, because the teacher actually touches the pupil and it's taught through contact. Talking about the work is not enough because you can talk yourself blue and no one will understand what you're talking about. So I use my hands. I've trained my hands to give the pupil a kinesthetic experience, a feeling in their bodies of what it is that I'm talking about. And it's not only a posture or a coordination that I'm encouraging, it's really a state of being, meaning that when one is freed physically, one feels open, responsive, emotionally available and ready for action. And I think that the most important part of what I teach is to make the actor ready to respond to whatever they're going to do. Unfortunately, a lot of people think of the Alexander technique as a postural training, and it really isn't. It's a way of organizing yourself for action. I always tell my actors this work will be good in your vocal training, in your acting class, and it will be good when you're working on a major film.

Whether it's on a one-to-one basis or in my group classes at UCLA, the work is the same. In the beginning, I usually ask my pupils to become aware of what's happening between the relationship of their heads to their bodies, because the basic principle of the Alexander technique is that there's a relationship between one's head and spine. And when there's too much pressure or stiffness in the neck, it pulls the head back and down into the spine, which compresses the whole spine and puts a lot of tension on the whole body. So with my hands and by talking to the pupil, I ask my student to free their neck to allow their head to go forward and up from the spine so the whole body can lengthen and widen. So with my hands, I'm encouraging very delicately that relationship they have to the spine, which in Alexander jargon we call the "primary control." Then I ask the pupil to think of something they want to do while I have my hands on them, for example, like standing from sitting or any kind of movement. And then I ask them not to respond right away to the movement because most people, if they respond quickly, they will pinch their neck again and pull down their heads and go back and down. But instead, I tell them, "Take a moment. Do not respond yet and think again of your direction, and while you're thinking of the direction, you can choose to just sit there and do nothing, or if you feel like it, you can begin to stand by taking this new coordination into the movement." So they learn about the place where they begin to revert to their habit, you see. And there's freedom when they can just continue to follow the direction and lead with their heads and lengthen each movement, because then they recognize that they can actually make a change. And I think my strength as a teacher is that I like to apply this new coordination to application. Basically, they'll bring in a monologue or a scene or a song, and I have them integrate this new coordination between their heads and bodies while they are acting.

Usually people call me and we have an initial conversation. I don't like to call it an interview, because I feel that the Alexander technique can be helpful for anyone. But I screen them in a way to make sure that I can help them. So I question them as to what their experience is, what their needs are, what they're expecting in terms of change and what their goals are in studying the Alexander technique. I also train teachers to teach the Alexander technique. I'm a training director and when we screen students to become teachers, it's very thorough in terms of making sure that the person knows what the Alexander technique is, whether they're capable to embody that and whether they have the patience. Patience is a big element, whether you're an actor or a teacher.

I practice the Alexander technique because I believe in it personally. I'm constantly changing, studying and learning. So when I teach, I'm learning myself. And I have a good time sharing it with my students. This work, after seventeen years, never gets stale for me because I am always in the space of wondering about the whole process—it's not something that I know all about, it's a work in progress I'm still learning about.

The Students of Jean-Louis Rodrigue

NATALIJA NOGULICH

I have learned from Mr. Rodrigue that my voice resonates through my entire body and that when I speak or perform an action, I can commit to it with my whole being. I am learning to feel free and unlimited in my use of myself on stage and unimpeded in my use of myself on camera. Mr. Rodrigue has helped me to own the space that I am playing in and given me a sense of dominion and empowerment.

Mr. Rodrigue has always been willing and available to work with me specifically on audition material or on role preparations. His vast knowledge of the theatre enables him to give educated assistance in classical and modern roles. He has also been generous in coming to the theatre and seeing me perform and helping me improve on a performance—his notes have always been supremely valuable.

Mr. Rodrigue is the single most powerful influence in my acting development. He has sensitivity, depth, expertise, understanding, and a great sense of joy and generosity of spirit. He also has amazing insight into individual needs for each student. I am so grateful to have been and continue to be a benefactor of his great love for the craft and his capacity to help me grow. He embraces the process and he has taught me to cherish the journey each step of the way.

JOSHUA WEBB

Jean-Louis has helped me detect and relieve tension from my body. In working with him, as I have explored the ways in which my body moves and functions and the ways in which my voice functions, I have become more aware and responsive. Jean-Louis is an extremely warm person and he has a lively sense of humor. He also knows how to communicate with actors quite well. I highly recommend Jean-Louis to any actor.

Jean-Louis Rodrigue: The Facts

Alexander Technique Performance Workshops
P.O. Box 3194
Beverly Hills, CA 90212
213-655-0016
310-395-9170

Also at:
UCLA School of Theater, Film and Television
405 Hilgard Avenue
Los Angeles, CA 90024

Length of time teaching: 17 years
Classes: At UCLA, classes are part of the three-year MFA Acting
   Program
   Weekly Group Classes
   Monday   6:30PM – 8:00PM
   Thursday   5:45PM – 7:15PM
Private Coaching: $55 per forty minutes
Admission: By private consultation

Chapter 22
DIANA STEVENSON

I worked in the theater when I was younger, actually, as a way to get out of classes in high school and after that, I began to work in Equity stock. So my first training really was from on-the-job experience. I went on to graduate from the American Academy of Dramatic Arts in New York. I also studied directing at HB Studio and I was a member of the American Mime Theater where I worked with Paul Curtis. But the greatest inspiration I received was from Phillip Burton who was Richard Burton's foster father. I had hit a point in my training where I felt everything was just a bit repetitive and his insights and views on Shakespeare was the exciting link for me. Although I had been reading Shakespeare since I was a child, I had never been enthusiastic about his plays. Phillip really opened up the potential of Shakespeare for me and he introduced me to a love of language that made all the difference.

I think my approach in training actors is a practical and common-sense one. I like to encourage in the actor a keen, objective observation of life. I don't encourage a great deal of introspection—I'm a bit leery of actors who find themselves far more interesting than any of the characters they're called upon to play. Of course self-interest is healthy and we must always start with who we are—that happens when we attempt to understand any other human being. But excessive self-interest easily becomes self-indulgence and I feel that's probably the single greatest impediment to fine acting. Actors need to move beyond the belief that acting is merely emotional accessibility and display. I accept that any actor possesses the full spectrum of basic human emotions he needs for his work, so I spend little time tampering with them. I guess I often shock students by stating at the beginning of class that feelings are the last thing we'll worry about. I'm usually forced to assure them that I never said we would not feel, I simply said it was the last thing we would worry about. And their relief is usually almost palpable in the classroom. As in life, I believe thinking does come first and I often point out that if we wish to surgically interfere with our emotional responses, it can be done by operating on the brain—not on some mysterious emotional center located somewhere between the chest and the belly.

I unashamedly stress text, subtext, and the application of imagery aligned to the illusion. I guess that leads me into the conflict I know is still going on with the divergent views as to the utilization of affective memory exercises. That's kind of a legacy of the fifties and sixties. I'm clearly on the side of those who feel that those are useful tools: emotional recall; sense memory; substitution—but not properly applied as actual reliable performance techniques. I see them as utilized in homework and rehearsal. I encourage the actor to find links or bridges from the understanding his life experiences provide to the images with which the character views his world and his path. I just want the actor's imagination to become legitimate again, to liberate him and to allow him into the illusion. I find so many actors are concerned about what feels comfortable and natural. But we're stretching for character; what's honest is what's honest for the character in the given circumstances, and I don't think that anything the actor does differently from the way he himself does it will feel comfortable automatically. I also have to warn actors that if they start to volunteer much about their private experiences, I'll probably run. I want them to use that to help in their understanding, but I don't necessarily want to be told about those things, and I'll return the favor. I'm not qualified as a therapist and I take that seriously. Like so many actors in the past, I've been worried about some of the things I've seen in acting classes when I feel that the teacher is in an area he or she is just not qualified to handle. I'm also concerned, and I know this is still more prevalent than I sometimes realize, that there are acting classes where if an actor breaks into tears, he's encouraged to think that he's made great advancement in his craft.

Most of the work I do is based on utilizing the scene, and it is structured more to learning how to rehearse. And out of rehearsal, then ultimately achieving final rehearsals and performance. After awhile my students get beyond the idea of performing for me and for their classmates and they suddenly realize a few sessions down the road that they are actually moving towards performance. It seems to be so difficult to get actors to accept that class is the place to test and try and fail and find your way— that it's a lab. I also require quite a bit of homework. I hate the term, but I don't suppose we've found a better one for that fifty per cent of an actor's work that's done doing research; finding everything he needs to know about the time and place; what's pertinent from the playwright's own experiences and other important elements. I also like to get into the issue of memorization because I think everything starts there. It's odd to me that we spend so little time and consideration on that. Traditionally, the actor just falls back on pure memorization like cramming the data for the biology exam or learning a speech to a local group. And I think he sets line readings rigidly, he interferes with his work by running lines incessantly and staring at pages and being prompted and paraphrasing and repeating dialogue in a monotone—which guarantees monotonous delivery and performance. So I do have other means, techniques to help the actor get the lines as written quite early, with the subtext fully incorporated.

My reputation with my students seems to be that my greatest emphasis is on text and maybe that's true. I don't necessarily plan it that way, I suppose it's just that my deep belief is that the play's the thing. I'm worried when an actor feels he can be judged favorably, independent of the play or his character. I find it so strange when actors come in with a point of view that the words are in the way of their creativity. I don't know whether that comes from having been presented with text as something dull and confining or limiting, but I try to go in the other direction to help the actor find out how much he's really set free to do his work by what's given in the text. To care for the text and dedicate himself to it; to dispose himself of prejudices and explore it with a fine-tooth comb and get every obvious point, every implication. I find this aspect of the work incredibly exciting and I enjoy sharing that excitement with my students.

The Students of Diana Stevenson

COLM O FAOLAIN

Diana is one of the most important persons in my life. If it was not for her kindness, love and support for me as an actor, I'd be a landscape designer. Diana has an unbelievable amount of knowledge and an uncanny way of knowing what each individual needs. I have learned from her the importance of doing my homework, how to listen and respond honestly and how to make the strongest possible choices. Simply, Diana is the greatest.

KIRSTEN CERRE

I chose Diana as a teacher because she has a no-nonsense approach and she explains the process of acting in clear, useful terms—not in vague or esoteric concepts. Diana has shown me how to enjoy speaking the English language. We bring poetry excerpts to class to work on "tasting" words by savoring vowels and biting into consonants. Also, Diana doesn't subscribe to a specific technique, but she encourages us to develop many different styles.

Diana is always available by phone to answer my questions and she has spent many hours coaching me to prepare for important auditions. Diana is a true professional and imparts to all of us how to be professional at all times.

MARGARET MAGNUSON

Diana has taught me many things so important to my growth as an actor. I have learned to trust and act upon my instincts, to make specific personal choices, to invest in my uniqueness and to be courageous enough to expand and explore. Diana also emphasizes the importance of research which has enabled me to serve the character's needs and the playwright's intent.

Diana never criticizes in a negative way, rather, her direction is always aimed at helping you find a solution. I consider Diana's instruction and guidance invaluable. I appreciate her high artistic standards, and because of them, I now have a disciplined, specific and self-reliant approach.

Diana Stevenson: The Facts

American Academy of Dramatic Arts
2550 Paloma Street
Pasadena, CA 91107
818-798-0777
818-848-8077

Length of time teaching: 18 years
Classes: Call for current schedule
Private Coaching: Variable fees, call for details
Admission: By interview and audition

Biography

LARRY SILVERBERG, author of *The Sanford Meisner Approach: An Actor's Workbook*, is a graduate of the Neighborhood Playhouse School of Theater in New York City where he studied with master acting teacher Sanford Meisner. Since then, he has worked professionally as an actor and director throughout the United States and Canada in feature films, network television, Off-Broadway, and regional theater. Most recently, Larry appeared with Tony LoBianco in the CBS series *Palace Guard*, in an award-winning production of Athol Fugard's drama *Hello and Goodbye*, and he has just completed directing *Shivaree* by William Mastrosimone.

Larry teaches professional classes in the Meisner work, both in his own acting studio and at the University of Washington. He has also taught Actors Master Classes at universities, colleges and acting studios around the United States. His students have gone on to work in TV and feature films including: *Cape Fear, Making Mr. Right, Let It Ride, Miami Vice, Northern Exposure, B.L. Stryker, Miami Blues, Super Boy, Phantom of the Ritz, America's Most Wanted* and many others. He also offers visiting master classes. You may contact him with questions about teaching at your school or about the content of this book at the following address.

Larry is the Founder and Artistic Director of the Belltown Theatre Center in Seattle, Washington. His address is: PO Box 16205, Seattle, WA 98116. (206) 781-7305.

The SANFORD MEISNER *Approach*

The best-selling workbook that opens the door to Meisner's Approach

"Here, Silverberg, who was a student of the master teacher, presents a workbook for actors that will prove useful, regardless of how familiar the reader is with Meisner's methods. Silverberg's writing is concise and insightful throughout and makes the technique accessible to any committed student."
—*Library Journal*

"For serious theatre students, this book could be highly influential in laying a foundation for their acting careers."
—*Voice of Youth Advocates*

includes specific exercises from the Method
ISBN 1-880399-77-6
176 pages $12.95

Published by Smith and Kraus
at your local bookstore or
call 1.800.895.4331